You Can't Cha...
Card: *13 Keys to Spiritual Power*

By Ayana Hinton

Mega Models Magazine, Inc. New York

"You Can't Charge Spiritual Debt to a Credit Card: 13 Keys to Spiritual Power," Copyright © 2012 by Ayana Hinton. Published by Mega Models Magazine, Inc. All rights reserved. Information address: P.O. Box # 130266, Brooklyn NY 11213. Email: info@ayanahinton.com Cover Art by Ayana Hinton. Cover Design and Layout by Kenneth Watson. ISBN: 978-0-615-75515-1

About the Author – I, Ayana Hinton am a Brooklyn, NY based author, life coach and artist. At the moment I am passionate about exploring issues that are misunderstood out of fear. I want to delve into those topics, then come back and share what I've learned so that we don't have to be afraid of something just because it is unknown.

Disclaimer: No part of this publication "You Can't Charge Spiritual Debt to a Credit Card: 13 Keys to Spiritual Power" may be reproduced, resold or transmitted in whole or part, without the written consent of the author. The author and publisher do not guarantee that the strategies recommended in this book will produce mirror- like results. The author will not assume liability for any unintentional errors or omissions. The author will not be held liable for any third party products or services mentioned as expressions of the author's opinion. In order to maintain their anonymity, the author may have changed some of the characters' identifying characteristics, properties and occupations. The events in this memoir are described according to the author's recollection and understanding of events.

I dedicate this book to YOU, dear reader. I hope it helps you get through whatever you may be going through. - Ayana Hinton

Acknowledgments - I thank The Creator for everything. I thank everyone mentioned in this book for giving me some of the most powerful, difficult and beautiful life experiences.

Contents

Chapter 1: The Road to Hell... 1

Chapter 2: Is Paved With Good Intentions ... 19

Chapter 3: Once Upon a Time 34

Chapter 4: Divine Intervention 55

Chapter 5: Reality Is Beautiful.......................... 71

Chapter 6: Lost On Vacation 84

Chapter 7: All That Glitters............................. 153

Chapter 8: Life Goes On................................... 187

Chapter 9: From Spiritual Debt to Spiritual Power... 207

Chapter 10: Living A New Story..................... 231

Chapter 1: The Road to Hell...

Is the purpose of life to find out what one's purpose in life is? Or, are we born with a sense of purpose already encrypted in us somewhere, encoded in our DNA? Is it possible to mine the spirit for leadership and guidance? If so, then how? And what does it mean when the spirit is not communicating with us or providing direction?

I've been called bold, careless and crazy but what I really had to be in order to survive *this* life is called courageous. I built my life as a bridge to escape from my past. There is nothing wrong with my being a little wild and unintentionally controversial. I love a good adventure so I take them pretty often in one way or another. But things have gotten way out of hand as of late and on more than one occasion. This path will lead me to either self-destruct or completely transform – the choice is mine.

People always ask me "What are you going to do?" That is the single most important philosophical question of our time. The way that each person answers that question is a reflection of their own inner world. An aggressive person will take action; a passive person will retreat into his or her own shell. But what would a normal person do when presented with life's challenges? What would you do? I did the best that I could under all kinds of circumstances, which brought out my wild side…

There I was, sitting in an office chair at a conference table in a long, cold, empty, beige room – with heather gray office carpeting, waiting alone. And I'm thinking to myself: *Oh no! Not again. Am I getting fired?* My stomach quivered. I took out a pen and scraped up a small piece paper from my handbag and quickly jotted down my thoughts about why what was about to happen was wrong. I had been a good worker. I was selected for the committee that worked on corporate ethics. I was the only worker in my department who was recognized by our auditors for the quality of my work. These are the things I wanted to tell them whenever they came into the room to drop the axe. *Dammit!* I was getting teary eyed.

I waited for what seemed like hours with a sick feeling in the pit of my stomach that was comparable to the feeling you get when you are alone in the waiting room of your dentist's office. Only you are next in line. Finally, the Executives came in. They shared a similar style of dress as many middle-aged women do, with low haircuts, flat black shoes and mid-calf length skirt suits. The color of one of their suits was graveyard grey and the other was dressed in punishment purple. They had blank facial expressions but tried to act concerned through the inflections of their voices, the same way I might have "tried" to sound sick when calling out of work. I wished I had called out today. Then again, it was pretty early in the morning so at least they'd fire me before lunchtime.

I had sat there in that freezing cold office and waited on them long enough for the fear in me to be morphed into a fiery anger. By now, I was dry eyed. I was ready for them but I don't think they were ready for *me*. Although they spoke to me, I didn't hear a word that they said. I was submerged in a sewer of negative thoughts and couldn't see my way out.

It would've been nice if I had actually said the words written on my paper. I wish I could tell you that I was professional and polite as I read from my little tear stained paper. But, no sooner than I was handed that letter of termination did I say something more to the effect of "Thank you for letting me go. Never before have I had the displeasure of working for incompetent house negroes like you! If the workers could evaluate you, then y'all would be getting fired today, not me!" Everybody knows that their office is rife with nepotism.

Then I snatched my termination letter off the table, told them I wasn't signing a damn thing and that they'd better have the paper work right for my unemployment insurance to kick in, ASAP. I stormed out of the conference room and on my way to the elevator, I saw the CEO of the company standing outside of her office door. It just so happened that I was headed in her direction, walking right towards her. I stopped dead and center in front of her face. I looked her in the eye and said "Are you happy? Are you happy now?!" She was speechless. Even though I was too upset to think of anything really clever to say, I was thrilled. I walked out of that dimly lit office building into a bright, sunny day with perfect weather, feeling free as a bird and quite happy for the first time in a long time knowing that I should have quit that job before they chewed me up and spit me out.

The first place I headed once I left the administrative building was to a vegetarian restaurant. It was within walking distance. I treated myself to what I would begin to consider as an expensive meal. Usually, vegetarian restaurants are pretty inexpensive. That was a different day in my world because I didn't know where my next meal was going to come from. The restaurant had Zen Buddhist décor and they always played really comforting lounge music. I held my head high and enjoyed my meal while carefully distracting myself with a book. I certainly did not want to ruin my appetite by reflecting on the morning's events.

After lunch, I felt totally clear - in fact I was crystal clear. I had gotten fired for being a whistleblower. It was out of character for me to have called those executives "house negroes" or to scream in the face of a corporate CEO. The reason I did so is because, let's face it, I was fired anyway and they were the persons to whom I had directly reported acts of corruption. My complaints were mysteriously leaked which unleashed a bevy of workplace hostility against me. In the end, my employment was terminated on the basis of the manner in which I had exposed the corruption. It doesn't require mental gymnastics to figure out why I had been let go.

As I headed home on the A train to my Brooklyn apartment, a sense of relief came over me. I had done the right thing, been honest and courageous in the face of no agreement. I did not have the support of the *vast* majority of my colleagues nor had I been protected by my supervisors or even *their* supervisors. In that "professional" environment I was first ignored, laughed at, then I was fought against. Based on everything I knew there was nowhere for me to go but, up.

In the meantime, the between time, I had to adjust to a new and different life. My life returned to the source, the infinite black field of possibility that I will refer to as "the drawing board." Obviously the central question was: *how would I survive without a paycheck?* Of course I filed for unemployment insurance; and of course my ex-employer disputed my claim. In other words, I wasn't getting any checks.

I am more than sure that my ex-employer and my ex-colleagues had easily written me off as "crazy." Considering that I had been nearly driven all the way to crazy while on the job, I was responsible enough for myself to have requested a referral from the Employee Program to see a real therapist. After three sessions, she looked me straight in the eye and said "quit the job, you can't change corporate culture." I was surprised that she offered such forthright advice. I was pleased to learn that I was not in fact crazy. I was just going along for the ride to "Crazy Town" and I didn't know where to get off the bus.

Adjusting to my new life inherently meant starting over, which required me to do this radical, new-agey thing called "looking within." I mean, I had a lot of time on my hands to reflect on the meaning of life but I no longer had the medical insurance to afford real therapy. The emotional weight of unresolved contradictions from a wrongful termination bogged me down mentally. The little voice in my head kept repeating itself like a broken record (or rather, a scratched CD) over the phrase: *They are wrong, you are right!* Yet I was not receiving any unemployment benefits while the treacherous "they" were seemingly off the hook.

The process of conducting a new job search was a whole other emotional roller coaster if nothing else. It consisted of hours of internet searches, cold calling, and fluctuations of excitement over promising prospects followed by deflations of disappointment over careless rejections. Apparently, that cycle was on wash, rinse and repeat too.

What I did not anticipate as a result of losing my job was the incredible feeling of "aloneness" that set in on me like cold air. In hindsight, I *did* have a handful of friends at work in that hell factory. At least it felt warmer to me there than being stuck at home having no job to go to at all. Furthermore, getting a regular paycheck enabled me to socialize with old friends in familiar places and make new friends in different places. Just the activity of commuting back and forth to work on a daily basis was a social act. Everyone that I knew had a job. I felt isolated by the lack of funds to go out and eventually found myself trapped in my own home. I isolated myself from the people who cared about me because when we would speak over the phone, they constantly asked me if I had found a new job yet and it was becoming increasingly difficult to keep telling them "No, not yet" over and over again.

In order to spare myself from repetitive conversations, I created the idea that people were making me feel uncomfortable. It was easy for me to say "you just don't get it," "he doesn't get it," "she doesn't get it," "they don't get it" or even in advance "they won't get it." "This isn't going anywhere because they just don't get it."

Of all my favorite complaints this one is at the top of my list: "All of this self-help crap I'm doing is just making my life harder." But was it making my life harder, or was it making my life easier? I was more easily upset and feeling incomplete because the truth was: I didn't get it. I didn't understand the elusive "it." "It's" the reason why my life wasn't working. Once again I was back at the drawing board, with the central question this time being: *Who am I?* Being unemployed only seemed to describe who I was not.

I did not have upbeat reports to give people which usually would have indicated that I was doing well in life. I was lost and had no desire to ask for direction from anybody that knew me. I was too embarrassed. And I would much rather hide from people than lie to them.

My character, while unemployed, was kind of like the story of "Rapunzel." I was locked up at home, just letting my hair grow while waiting for someone or something miraculous to come and rescue me from the tower. The only outside contact I was making happened over the phone and internet during my job search. There was no particular person that I craved the attention of. Still

I felt alone, as in isolated. It was my choice to cut people off once I became unemployed. However it was still difficult to be alone. I noticed the sudden death of my social life. My phone stopped ringing and there were no visitors.

Being home alone was beginning to bore me, the silence was deafening. Depression became my friend. When I had control of my thoughts, in between those moments where the negative little voice in my head would define the nature of my reality, all I could think was: *how am I going to survive? I have to eat, pay rent, pay bills and oh my God – STUDENT LOANS!* Yes, I have the infamous "student loans," from earning my Master's Degree in Business Administration (MBA) from a private school. I was haunted by the fear of impending debt and I would be visited by many of its ghosts, the debt collectors.

Unfortunately, I could not depend on any support from my family. In difficult times, I can only recall the simple fact that I was orphaned at the age of 4 by living biological parents. Additionally, my extended family had left me alone, feeling rejected and abandoned. I grew up as a "ward of the court." Aside from the fact that none of my immediate family members lived in my state, I had not been in communication with them for long periods of time. My mother, father, older sister and younger brother were disinterested in and disconnected from me even when I was doing well in life. I had been their stable support system and connection to each other for the past 10 years or more, but I was still always left and expected to make it on my own.

On the other hand, it was totally normal in my view for me to be on my own. I had mastered the art of living alone, having done it successfully since the age of 18 when I signed myself out of the foster care system. At the time I could have stayed in the system until I was 21. But I was pretty worn out after being been shuffled around in at least 10 different foster homes and 2 group homes starting from the age of 4, so I dreamt long and hard of being on my own as soon as I turned 18. And now, for the first time in my adult life I was faced with the prospect of being homeless as a result of being unemployed.

I'm pretty sure you've heard the old saying that "God takes care of babies and fools." Well, I prefer to think of myself as a thirty-something year old baby but it wasn't too long after losing my job that I began to act like a damn fool.

One restless night, I went outside around 11pm. I intended to buy a few food items from the local bodega a few days before a massive storm was set to hit NYC. On my way to the store I ran into a female who I hadn't seen since I was 15 years old. We lived in the same group home together as teenagers. She recognized me first but she still looked the same so I recognized her too. I was happy to see her and we embraced. She was standing outside of a seedy nightclub. She said that she was about to go in there and have a few drinks. She asked me to join her in the nightclub but I instead offered to purchase a bottle of alcohol and invited her into my apartment just around the corner so that we could sit down, have a drink and catch up. She accepted my offer. We stayed up until nearly 4:00 AM drinking vodka and talking about old times.

I watched as she popped a couple of large, white pills. When I tried to warn her that she shouldn't take her prescription along with the alcohol we were drinking, she just waved me off and said her pills weren't prescribed... she'd bought them off the street.

I dared not ask what she was taking. I certainly didn't want any parts of it. I was getting pretty smashed off the vodka. It was pineapple flavored and we were drinking it straight, with no chaser. The large bottle that I purchased normally would have lasted me a few days; instead we drank the whole damn thing in one sitting.

I remember that she cried on my shoulder while telling me that she had just come out of an abusive relationship. She also disclosed that she had recently been arrested and was out on bail at the moment. The tears welled up in her eyes and rolled down her cheeks as she told me that her family had turned their backs on her over the years all because she was the darkest skinned member of her family. I was sympathetic, I allowed her to cry on my shoulder. I hugged her and patted her on the back. She talked about God and told me how blessed I was.

She told me that I had always been a strong person when we were growing up. She reminisced about how I used to call her into my room and tell her to stop getting into trouble, to go to school and get herself together. At the time, I didn't want to be just another person to judge her so I didn't hold any of the things that she said against her. I knew it was time for her to leave my apartment but I did not want to send her out into the dark morning at 4:00 AM while she was vulnerable, drunk and crying.

That is the point where I ignored not one, but **two** lessons that I had previously learned. First of all, (and I know that this is ironic but) one of my hallucinogenic meditations had informed me to stop drinking alcohol several years ago. I had been told what to do in previous meditations. Each meditation brought me one or more lessons. It was up to me to implement those lessons without having to go through the growing pains of learning them the hard way.

Second of all, I had memorized a lesson that I got from watching Oprah Winfrey because she often quotes Maya Angelou as saying "when people tell you who they are, believe them." So here I was getting drunk with someone who told me that she had consistently been on a downward spiral for the past 16 years since the last time I had seen her. During that time period I had started a clothing line, earned an MBA degree and seen the world. However, what did I do in the moment? I got caught up. I told her that it was almost 4:00 AM and that she could just sleep on my living room sofa because I was too drunk to continue the conversation.

I went to my bedroom and left her in my living room. Once in bed, I totally blacked out. I woke up in a foggy, daze about four hours later around 8:00 AM. My vision was very blurry. I turned over to get up and shockingly - there was a man in my bed. I jumped up, he remained asleep. I looked down and touched my body. I still had my dress on. I got out of my bed, left him there and went out into the living room looking for my girl "friend."

There was broken glass all over the living room floor, along with a random pair of panties, two used condoms and their empty wrappers. The large bottle of vodka that I had bought the night before was empty lying on the floor as well. And as for my "friend," she was gone. Not only was she gone but so was my pocketbook, my Nintendo Wii system, the controllers, and all of my games for the Wii console. I was flabbergasted.

I went back into my bedroom where the strange man was still asleep in my bed, noticing that some of my expensive perfumes had also gone missing from my dresser. All I had was questions with no answers running through my mind. I woke him up and asked what his name was. He gave me a nickname like a street name.

I asked him whether or not we'd had sex. He said that he tried to have sex with me but that I refused him. He also said that my now absent "friend" had invited him over to my place. I had no recollection. But I did not *feel* physically like I had *been* physically penetrated down there. Those empty condom wrappers on the floor were Magnums so I would have felt physically sore if he had penetrated me during my black out. How I felt mentally was another story. As calmly and politely as I could, I asked him to leave. He left without any dispute. I called the police.

When they arrived, I told the police that an old female friend had stolen from me as I slept. The police said that if I had not witnessed her stealing my possessions with my own two eyes then I could not prove that she had in fact stolen those items from me. The cops said that she could've left my apartment door open when she left and a neighbor could've wandered into my apartment and stolen those things from me as I slept. I was greatly disappointed but what could I say? As the police were leaving they told me to cancel all of my credit cards since my pocketbook had been stolen.

In the process of cancelling one of my credit cards, I found out that before I had even woken up at 8am that morning to learn that she had stolen from me, my so-called friend had gone home and charged her utility bills to one of my credit cards. The only good thing about this was that it was the type of proof needed by the police to formally make an arrest and charge her with a crime.

She went on to spend three weeks in jail and the next year of her life going back and forth to court with that charge and the charge that she had caught a few weeks before she and I bumped into each other- destruction of property, how fitting. Needless to say, she was already on probation before she caught these two charges.

The theft incident was traumatic enough but it would not be the last time I would see her around my neighborhood and have to call the police on her ratchet ass. One evening I was approaching the corner store, literally around the corner from my place, and "she" approached me out of nowhere saying that she wanted to pay me back for the things that she had stolen from me but since the case was still pending in the court system she didn't want to risk violating the court order of protection against her. Just the simple fact that she approached me in public was a violation of the order of protection. Everything that I had wanted to say to her since the incident first happened came rushing to the surface and spilled out of my mouth:

"Fuck you bitch! You got what you deserved! You sat in jail for like three weeks you stupid fucking bitch! Was it worth it? No it wasn't worth it, was it? I bet not you piece of shit! Where is my shit? Where is my fucking Wii and my games? Where is my leather pocketbook and my MK shades that were inside of it? You stole my pocketbook, my reading glasses! I had money from Brazil, Europe and Jamaica inside that wallet bitch, you can't replace that!"

Strangely, she listened and nodded her head in agreement until I was finished. Then she pretty much said "God is gonna punish me. I did think about what I did when I was in jail. You was nice to me. I don't know why did that. I know that God is going to punish me for what I did to you but all I can do right now is just try to pay you back and make amends."

I wanted to knock her head off but I knew that the case was still pending so I told her it would cost me $400 to replace my reading glasses and that she could give that money to a middleman. I reminded her that she had been popping pills that night and that she probably robbed me because she was a drug addict. I demanded to know if she had slipped me a mickey and if she had sex with the dude she left behind because she had left her panties on my living room floor with two used condoms next to them. I was really hoping to get confirmation that the two of them had sex and left me out of it.

Suddenly, a young black male approached us. He was tall, dark and ugly. His hair looked messy like he had not had a hair cut in months. He looked skinny, scraggly and like a strung out drug addict. He immediately stepped in my face and said "watchu doing to my mother?"

Apparently, he had been inside of the corner store as I was approaching it, which would explain why she was standing outside of it when I walked up. I looked him up and down and I told him "your mother robbed my house, if you got a new Wii, she stole it from me." He shook his head in disbelief, "I don't believe you," he said.

He was wearing a puffy jacket and suddenly with both of his hands he gripped the bottom of the jacket, yanked it up and showed me a metallic handle that was either a small handgun or a large knife. I did not show my fear. In similar style, I threw one of my hands into my coat pocket and whipped out my cell phone, without breaking eye contact with him. I nervously (and without looking) mis-dialed 911 at least five times before I got it right. Thank God they answered instead of sending me to a pre-recorded message.

As the good thief's son was in my face with his hand on a weapon that was in the waist of his pants, I was on speakerphone with a 911 operator:

"This is 9-1-1. What is your emergency?"

"I'm on the corner of blank and blank streets and this guy is threatening me with a weapon. I can't tell exactly what it is but it's either a gun or knife because the handle is a shiny black metal. I have an order of protection against this girl that approached me and now her son is threatening me!"

Immediately after I said that, the thief shouted "She's calling the police! She's calling the police!" She yanked her son away from me and they took off running around the corner while I stood still on the phone with the 911 operator. In less than 5 minutes, NYPD was on the scene asking questions and such but it was too late. They escorted me home but nothing else came of it. A year after robbing my apartment and charging her cable bill to my stolen credit card, she pled guilty to disorderly conduct in my case and I received an extended order of protection.

Chapter 2: Is Paved With Good Intentions

It was now two months into my unemployment with no source of income or any new job prospects on the horizon. I was still reeling from the trauma of having betrayed myself, by drinking myself into a coma, thereby enabling an old "friend" to rob me and leave me for dead with a strange male in my bed. I decided to stop drinking alcohol for good this time. I tried to look on the bright side. I was grateful to have escaped from the situation(s) with my life. I could eventually replace the things that were stolen. I was even happier about the things that were not stolen! There were other items lying around that were left behind like my cell phone, 2 lap tops, digital camera and iPod which were more important and valuable to me than the things that were actually stolen from me.

Most broken was my heart, I can't believe that I trusted this person and it would take a long time before I could trust anyone again. *The only way to be safe was to be alone,* became a logical assumption. If this is what it took for me to stop drinking, then so be it. I had been drinking alcohol socially throughout my entire adult life and was at the point of consuming alcohol at least 3-4 times per week when I was employed. My drinking had escalated to this level of frequency as a result of stress from my old job. I used to keep a bottle in the cupboard and take a shot after bed time some nights when the anxiety from having to return to a hostile work environment the next day, kept me up at night.

There were many other opportunities to have a drink including happy hour after work with colleagues, or when catching up with old friends, clubbing on weekends, purchasing alcohol whenever I had guests over… Drinking alcohol was normal among my friends. I did not properly evaluate the consequences of quitting alcohol cold turkey before I decided that I was actually going to do it. I did not consider that I had been drinking a few times per week for the past two years. I just decided to speed up my emotional healing process by doing something positive for myself.

I really thought I was being responsible for my health. So I did not connect the dots when two short days after I stopped drinking I started to have migraine headaches, insomnia at night and nightmares during the day. I kept dreaming about being attacked while I lay motionless in bed watching my attacker advance towards me and knowing his intent, but not being able to move – it was the same dream every single time I drifted off to sleep. I would wake up sweaty all around my neck. As if insomnia and sweaty daytime nightmares were not enough to keep me off balance, a totally and completely overwhelming sense of fiery **rage** had come over me like a cloud of thick, black smoke. I could not see my way out of it. I had shut everyone out of my life so there was no place to direct the latent anger of my past except towards myself.

Overall, I had started drinking alcohol in high school with my peers when I was about 16. There was a lot of emotional turbulence in my life then. I had been in the foster care and group homes for 12 years by that time. Once I started drinking, I stopped counting the years of baggage I was accumulating and started forgetting about the baggage I had already incurred. So the baggage of a lifetime was always there but I just wasn't dealing with any of it in my daily awareness. This baggage was coming to the surface unannounced and uninvited now that I was officially detoxifying myself from alcohol.

I felt so enraged, frustrated and angry that I wanted to pull my hair out. I'd want to hit somebody. I wanted to release the pent up energy. Four days into my self-imposed detoxification from alcohol – I didn't want alcohol - I wanted to commit suicide. But then I would think: *Today is not **the** day*. Well, I couldn't really bring myself to actually kill myself but it was becoming a recurring thought. The **raaaage** I was feeling had no end and the stress that it caused me to feel also had no end until killing myself seemed like the only option to be free of the endless rage. After three straight days of repetitive suicidal ideations I tried to distract my restless mind by turning the television on.

A commercial was in progress that spoke directly to me, it was for a suicide prevention hotline. At the end of the commercial, I decided to pick up the phone before it was too late. I called the national suicide hotline and told my truth: "Help me... I'm drowning."

Was being unemployed and $100,000 in mostly student loan debt a major factor in my reasoning for contemplating suicide? You're damn right it was. But only about 30% of my stress had come from the inability to pay my debts. The remaining 70% of my stress mountain came from lack of spiritual work. Communion with God as a lifestyle includes: talking to God (prayer) and listening to God (meditation.) From my prayers and meditations I had been given a purpose. When I am living on purpose, I am walking with God. When I am not living on purpose, I am walking away from God. God does not leave us – we leave God. Then we wonder where God has gone. Then we wonder who we are.

So there I was, all choked up on the phone with a suicide prevention specialist. I could barely speak through the tears. The operator was pleasantly present but he wasn't indulgent. He gave me a safety plan. He was really straight with me about the feelings and behaviors that I was engaging in which perpetuated suicidal thoughts. He had me make a list of coping mechanisms that I could realistically act on and he gave me referrals to professional resources.

For the next two weeks I received random phone calls from different staff members of the national suicide hotline who were calling to check up on me and pretty much make sure that I was still alive. They left voice mails for me when I didn't answer the phone. They would make small talk with me when I did answer the phone. At some point I perked up and convinced the representative that I was going to be OK and the calls stopped. But I have to say, now in retrospect, that those calls saved my life. Thank you, LIFENET.

Although I didn't know it at the time, most of my symptoms were synonymous with alcohol withdrawal: headaches, insomnia, nightmares, sweats, spasms and overwhelming floods of emotion. I would now advise anyone with long term alcohol use, even if it's just social use, to detoxify under medical supervision. However, my suicidal ideations were not unique to this occasion. Even though I had succeeded in accomplishing my life plan, truly completing everything that I set out to do before I turned 30 my plan obviously didn't work. Because even after completing the plan for my life, I came close to committing suicide. This self-imposed alcohol detox had resulted in my second battle with suicide.

The first time I ever contemplated it is when I was only eight years old while living in a foster home with my brother who is 4 years younger than me. The foster parent would spank us pretty often. Sometimes it was for a reason and sometimes for no reason at all. One time I ate some imitation Oreo cookies. I would pull the cookie apart to scrape the icing from the middle of the cookie on to my teeth and eat it. But then I would throw the rest of the cookie, the hard outer parts, under my bed. When my foster mother found those cookie bits under my bed she told me to get down on my knees and pick them up. Afraid as I was, I complied with her. I sunk down to my knees looking up at her as if to say: *I know the storm is coming, what are you going to do to me now?*

Before I could even bend over on the floor to reach my arm under the bed and pull out the cookies she angrily grabbed me by my hair at the back of my head and started to slam my forehead into the hardwood floor over and over again while yelling that I had better get those cookies out from under the bed. It seemed like every word ended with my face being slammed into the floor: "YOU.

Bam! BETTER. *Bam!* GET. *Bam!* THOSE. *Bam!* COOKIES. *Bam!* OUT. *Bam!* FROM. *Bam!* UNDER. *Bam!* THE. *Bam!* BED. *Bam!*

Granted it wasn't the first time that she had physically abused me but it was the worst time that I can remember. When my little brother and I would go to the Foster Care agency once a week to visit with our mother in a supervised setting I would tell my mother and the social worker that our foster mother was beating us. The social worker would confront our foster mother in front of me with my side of the story. The foster mother would break out into a wide grin, showing all of her teeth like a wolf, and say "I love these kids! I would never beat them. She's lying." Then she would laugh out loud.

This happened week after week after week with my foster mother beating me severely when we got home because I had told on her. Eventually the social worker gave me a notebook and told me to write down each time that the foster mother spanked me or my little brother. Like clockwork, as soon as we got home the foster mother snatched that note book away from me. She hit me in the head with it a few times then she threw it on the floor and started hitting me all over with her hands slapping, punching, pushing, shoving, and pulling me by the neckline of my shirt until I fell limp. I never saw the notebook again nor did the social worker ever ask me about it again.

It was around this time that I decided to take action: go into the bathroom, look in the medicine cabinet and swallow the entire contents of the first bottle of pills that I saw. There happened to be a bottle of 120 tablets of aspirin in her medicine cabinet. I popped the top up with my thumb, poured the aspirin into my mouth and washed it down with mouthfuls of tap water. I repeated the process until the bottle was empty. I didn't want to be found unconscious on the bathroom floor because I didn't want to risk being revived. So I left the apartment without telling anyone.

I got into the elevator and headed for the lobby. I thought it would be better to go outside for walk – it was dark outside so I could find a place maybe in the grass where I could lie down comfortably, unnoticed and die. This way I would be really, really dead before they found my body.

My destiny awaited me. As I entered the elevator, I began to feel extremely nauseous. I pressed the lobby button, the doors closed and the elevator quickly jutted downward. The rise in my stomach that occurred as a result of the elevator suddenly descending made me vomit everything that I had just swallowed down a few minutes before. By the time I looked up I had reached the lobby but I was standing in a pool of my own vomit and it looked exactly like 100 scattered pills on top of a small puddle of water. I was so embarrassed to have failed and even worse I was afraid of the consequences. Quickly, I pressed button number 14 and rode the same elevator right back up to the floor that I had caught the elevator from. I returned to the apartment where my foster mother lived which was also the place that made me want to die.

Back to the drawing board, I constructed a new plan. This time I was going to lay my life down on the line by doing something really bad. I knew that she sold Mary Kay products. I knew that we were not allowed to touch her suitcase of makeup. One day I pulled her massive case of makeup out, opened all of the tubes and squeezed their contents out all over the inside of the makeup case. Some of the tubes had a pretty blood red color coming out of them. Almost instinctively I rubbed this thick, rich red color all over my palms like lotion, then I walked over to the wall, red handed, and placed both of my stained palms on the walls in about five different places. I was very happy with myself and satisfied with my work.

I had single-handedly (more like double-handedly) destroyed her beloved make up case, I had enjoyed myself playing with her blood red make up and to top it all off I got to stain her walls with my red hand prints. I washed my hands thoroughly. I hid the make-up case away. Then my evil foster mother came home. She saw the red marks on the walls and immediately charged towards my 4 year old little brother. He was watching cartoons.

She grabbed him by the wrist and dragged him into the living room where I had done my damage, unbeknownst to him. She grabbed me by the wrist from where I was sitting on the couch already in the living room, so as to give myself away, and dragged me over to the wall. She was screaming at the top of her lungs "Who did this? Which one of you did this?" I was speechless. I was scared. I was scared for my little brother. I was scared for myself. I didn't anticipate this. I had just assumed that she would automatically blame me and that this would be the straw to break the camel's back, for me.

What was happening was totally out of my control and because I didn't plan it this way I had to re-strategize in the moment. Since neither he nor I said anything I started to hope that neither one of us would get in trouble. She took one of my little brother's hands and placed his palm against one of my red hand prints on the wall. Then she took one of my hands in placed my palm against one of the red hand prints. Unsatisfied with her little hand test, she again held my brother's hand up to one of the makeup marks on the wall and she did the same thing again with my hand. After measuring each of our hands against the markings on the wall twice the foster mother concluded that it was my little brother who had gotten into her make-up case and put these blood red hand prints all over her wall.

Without any warning she smacked my little brother down to the ground. She was a heavy set woman, yet she got on top of him and mercilessly smacked him around pretty bad. He was just a little kid about four or five years old at the time. I found his screams and cries to be intolerable. It brings tears to my eyes even now. I wanted this to be the last beating that I would ever get from her. But I found myself unable to say that it was me who deserved that beating. I still feel guilty about that to this day. It wasn't my intention for him to be punished on my behalf. That day I remained silent but in my mind I became even more determined to get revenge.

This time I had to form a more serious plan of attack. I'd been through hell and back in this foster home. The foster mother's 2 adult children lived in the apartment with us. My little brother shared a bedroom with her adult son. I found her son's secret stash of crack rocks and handed it over to her. They were packaged inside small red topped tubes. At the time I didn't know exactly what it was although I did look inside of the brown paper bag, but she sure cursed him out pretty terribly when he came home that evening and she confronted him with it. Little did she know he was selling drugs right out of her apartment and that when she was at work during the day he would have more than one crack addicted female in the apartment on the living room couch under a blanket having sex with him. He would tell me that it was his girlfriend but I knew that it wasn't always the same woman that he was with under that blanket.

And then there was her grown daughter with whom I shared a bedroom, where in the bed next to mine she would have sex with her boyfriend. I was miserable. I didn't see a way out. So I did the *next* thing that came to mind. One day when none of the adults were home I went into my foster mother's bedroom and went through her dresser drawers. I found some envelopes that contained her billing statements and the cash that it would take to pay the each of the bills off. There were about five envelopes altogether with cash and billing statements inside of them. I took them all into the bathroom, put them in the sink and set them on fire. I left the burnt money and paper there in the sink for her to find them just like that - "fubar" (fucked up beyond all recognition.)

Then she came home and finally, just like that, she packed up all of my belongings and all of my little brother's belongings into a black garbage bag and drove us back to the Foster Care agency. She never asked who did it or why. She didn't spank either one of us this time. She didn't even yell. She was uncharacteristically quiet, peaceful even. She left us in the lobby at the receptionist's desk without even bothering to call our social worker down. Little did either one of us know that I would live to see her again.

It just so happened that I went to High School in the same neighborhood where the abusive foster mother lived when I was eight years old. One day after school I went to her apartment by myself. I was curious to see if she was still boarding foster children. The elevator ride was eerie, the nostalgia was nauseating. She recognized me as soon as she opened the door. With a wide, wolf toothed smile she backed up and welcomed me in.

I was in a daze as I crossed that threshold. I had no feelings at all. I didn't feel angry, sad or happy. Still I managed to say, "I was wondering if you had any old pictures of me and my brother from when we were little." She just laughed and said she would not be able to find any pictures at the moment. I asked f her if I could see my old bedroom, the one I had shared with her adult daughter.

She allowed me to go to the room by myself. I opened the door and peaked in, there were three small children sleeping —two kids on a bunk bed and a third child on a miniature single bed. Those children seemed to be between the ages of 4-6. I would have spoken to them, asked them if they were ok, but they were either asleep or pretending to be asleep.

When I went back to the front of the apartment, near where I had entered, the foster mother started to bring up some of the most awkward old memories. She kept grinning in an odd fashion, showing her glistening teeth like a rabid wolf. Out of nowhere she says, "Remember how *bad* you used to be?" I looked at her but did not reply, I was too busy eyeing the exit in my peripheral view. She continued, "One time I told you to wash the dishes. When I took a glass off the dish rack it was so greasy that it slipped out of my hand and busted up all over the kitchen floor."

I laughed out loud. *I can't believe this bitch has the audacity to bring this crap up.* I kept my thoughts to myself. I said to her, "Look, I was only eight years old then and I didn't know how to wash dishes so I just rinsed them off in the sink and put them on the rack to dry." She wasn't done, instead she says, "I remember when I told you to go get me something to drink and you put bleach in my soda."

I replied, "No, I don't remember that but I guess you were trying to kill me and I was just trying to get your ass first." The silence that followed my statement was deafening but it was also a defining moment. There I stood at 16 years old, 5'11 and over 200 pounds. She was fatter than me, but I had a height advantage over her. Just staring into her eyes, for a prolonged moment before I left, clarified that I was no longer afraid of this woman and that she could never physically harm me again. I wished I could say the same for the three kids she now had living with her.

Chapter 3: Once Upon a Time

Before the point of losing my job, being denied unemployment insurance, getting robbed and nearly losing my will to live, I was used to having it all under control. I really could depend on myself before I turned 30. I made a life plan and I worked it out. My plan started with working from the age of 14, saving my money, graduating early from high school, launching a clothing line, earning a college degree, travelling to 6 countries and capping it all off by earning an MBA degree. And the only catch was that I wanted to do it all before the age of 30. I accomplished it all by the age of 28. The only restrictions I placed on myself were that I would not have children out of wedlock nor would I ever do synthetic drugs.

Having children was never in the plan unless I either got married or could afford to raise them on my own. I saw how devastating it was to have a child within failing relationships through my own observation of other women's lives, so I decided to stick with my plan by learning from theirs.

At 17 years of age I was in my first semester of college, and still living in the group home while working at a fast food restaurant. Even as a freshman, I was very active in black student union clubs. One of my favorite clubs was the gospel choir, of which I was a member. However, in order to maintain integrity with my life plan and keep myself under my own self- imposed parental control, I had an abortion during my freshman year.

Although I never confided in any of the members of the choir that I had an abortion, I received their forgiveness for it in a dream. After the medical procedure, I felt really woozy because I had been under anesthesia. With no one to claim me, I took a cab home, got in bed and fell into a deep sleep. Even though I had that dream so many years ago I can still recall it to this day. I dreamt that I walked onto my college campus looking for the gospel choir's rehearsal room. When I found it, the members of the choir gathered around me and presented me with a long white box that had a red ribbon on top of it. I opened the box and it contained a dozen, long stemmed, red roses. I accepted the roses with tears of gratitude. When I woke up the next morning I interpreted my dream as a sign of forgiveness from God.

There was something about being in college, six months ahead of my peers, that made me feel like an adult. I plotted my escape from the group home day and night. People came and went in that environment like a revolving door. I encountered at least 50 different girls and 20 different staff workers, managers and social workers over the course of 5 years. I was the only constant resident in this whirlwind of people who were entering the group home. There was one staff member that also remained constant. She taught me how to cook for a whole family, clean an entire house, sew my own clothes and crochet blankets. She also made me feel like a human being. Every Easter she would give me a very traditional but hand packed, basket full of candy, it made me feel young and loved.

On the weekends, all or most of the girls in my group home would go home to visit their parents, I was left alone. It was very rare that I would have a place to go on the weekends. For the most part I stayed in at the group home and did all of the chores in the house. This is how I learned to clean a house. Once per week each girl in the house, there were six of us, had to cook for the whole house. That is how I practiced cooking. But something has to be said for this one staff member in particular, and she knows who she is, because she instilled morals, values and discipline in me. Aside from the Easter baskets, she would buy me expensive gifts and even go out of her way to replace personal items of mine that would get stolen by the fly-by-night girls who came and went in and out of the group home on a regular basis.

At least 95% of the girls left the group home pregnant only to get transferred to another group home for pregnant girls, then they got dumped into public shelters until they eventually wound up in some form of public housing. The other 5% left the group home as run-aways going to live with their boyfriends or simply disappearing into the unknown. I was totally unique in that way, I signed myself out of the foster care system as a sophomore in college, because I felt like an adult and had saved enough money to move into my own apartment. And then I was *really* on my own.

From the classified section of a news paper, I found a one bedroom apartment rental unit for $450. However, it was so small I had sleep in the living room, on a futon that doubled as a bed and couch because the designated "bedroom" was no bigger than a closet. Welcome to Brooklyn - it was all that I could afford.

The neighbors who lived on the right side of my first floor apartment were a married couple, with 4 young children. On my left side, the neighbor was a really young drug dealing guy, in his twenties, who would leave his apartment door open at night and blast his music. There would be a parade of people going in and out of his apartment all night. He frequently hosted fish fry nights, card games and football parties at his place. Sometime he would knock on my door and invite me over, but his friends were too rowdy for me to get involved with so I would politely decline. I just didn't understand why he had to leave his front door open while his parties were going on well into the wee morning hours.

I devoted more and more of my time and attention into the Black Student Union clubs at my school. I was no longer participating in the gospel choir, there was way too much internal fighting going on so our choir never consolidated itself enough to travel as a group or compete nationally against other choirs as was the original intent of the choir. So I quit the choir and started to spend more time within the Black Student Union clubs. My affiliation with the Black Student Union started to affect my mental attitude. I cut my chemically permed hair off and began to grow my hair naturally. I found that wearing my hair all natural suits me quite well.

More often than not, I wore original clothing designs that I made for myself to school. It got me noticed by a lot of people. When students would ask me where I got my clothing, I would tell them that I made it. Soon, I was asked to participate in a fashion show that would raise money for one of the student clubs. I was flattered that several people thought highly enough of my personal clothing to expect me to deliver a full clothing line worthy of a fashion show. I wound up doing two fashion shows for the student club. One was held on campus in the auditorium and the other was held in the ballroom of a hotel. I was proud of myself for putting in the extra work late at night to produce my first clothing line.

Without even planning it in advance, I created a new identity for myself through my new hair, self-made clothing and the lessons I took in through my studies of African-American history and culture. My degree major was Psychology. Learning about the inner workings of the human mind intrigued me more than anything else. Other areas I studied were: Education, Sociology, Women's Studies and Philosophy. I was spending so much time on campus that I was asked to become an event planner for the Black Student Union. It was my responsibility to book speakers and catering for the on-campus annual celebrations of Black History Month, Black Solidarity Day and Kwanzaa. I enjoyed listening to all of the speakers. I wondered why they couldn't all get together and be a part of the same ONE organization. They each had good view points, but no one was willing to work together beyond the panel discussions. Everyone wanted to do their own thing.

I knew there was more to life than "the Black experience" and I was determined to find out what else there was. I started to converse with students who had varying religious beliefs. I bought lots of books on everything from old world religions to new age spirituality. The new age stuff seemed to stick to me the most so I became Buddhist. But it was a textbook type of Buddhism that I practiced. I didn't bring my spirituality to Buddhism; I superimposed Buddhism over my spirituality.

My parents had been Rastafarian, which is based on the Ethiopian Bible. But throughout the years of my being in multiple foster homes I was made to visit nearly every denomination of King James Bible based religions. I remember attending religious services at The Kingdom Hall of Jehovah's Witnesses, a Catholic Church, Christian sects: Baptist, Methodist, Episcopalian, Pentecostal, and Non-Denominational. My favorite religious experiences were within Baptist and Non-Denominational churches. In the Baptist church there were a lot of musical celebrations and Sunday brunches. In the Non-Denominational church they had a "come as you are policy" so I could go to church in my jeans and sneakers and so would everyone else. Youth members of the church, including myself were taken to Christian camp in the summer.

Summer camp with the church was an amazing and positive experience for me. The camp grounds were called "Lake Champion" and it was run by Christian volunteers. It was a beautiful forest retreat with plenty of entertainment for young people. There was a lake with row boats, zip lines, canoes and paddle boats. I remember this massive inflated tube on the lake that kids took turns jumping on and then bouncing off of it into the lake. There was a swimming pool, outdoor hot tub and indoor games like pinball, table top tennis, fuse ball and table top pool. They had various obstacle courses set up like the "American Gladiator," television show, there was even a rock climbing wall.

Coming from the jungle of skyscrapers that is NYC, it was a really cool experience for me to be able to take walks out into the forest and look up at the trees. The head rush you get from looking up so far is kind of weird but that's the view of nature we get from the ground. We are all used to having our feet planted firmly on the ground so imagine my horror when I was pressured to complete an aerial tightrope walk. I remember crying my way through this obstacle course that was literally set up in the tree tops and anchored by the branches.

First I had to put a harness on around my waist, then climb a little bitty 40 feet into the air. My harness fit like snug underwear over my jeans and it was connected to a high wire above my head so if I fell off the aerial obstacle course, I wouldn't plunge down 40 feet to my death, instead I would be left hanging in the air with no other choice but to get back on the tight rope beneath my feet, grip on to each wire on my left and right hand sides and continue to inch toward the next tree top that was at least 10 yards ahead.

I am afraid of heights so it wasn't until my second summer visit to Lake Champion that I decided to take on the tree top obstacle course challenge. Instinctively, I knew that it would be my last time camping at Lake Champion. I did most of the course with my eyes closed, tears streaming down my face. There were encouraging Bible quotes posted on each tree that you made it to before you got to the last one. The trees were few and far between the high wires. Putting one foot in front of the other on thin, metal rope seemed impossible even as I was engaged in doing it. I was totally pulling myself forward using the cables in my left and right hands with each step. Looking down was not a savory option.

At the last tree top in the course, I had to sit on a short plank of wood, way up in the air and remove my harness in order to put on a different one. It was an intimate space that relied on trust. For a few moments I'd have no harness on to prevent a sudden and tragic death drop. But I managed to wiggle out of one harness and into another, minus the humpty-dumpty fall. The instructor double checked my harness to make sure it was secure then he told me to count to three.

I shouted out loud "One! Twooooooooo....." and he shoved my back off that little plank (the thin line between life and death) into a 35 foot bungee style, free fall drop that left me swinging between the trees until someone on the ground caught me and unhooked me from my harness. With my feet planted firmly on the ground once again, I patted myself on the back for confronting my fear of heights head on. I needed to pat myself on the back to make sure that I wasn't a ghost and that my spirit was in fact, still inside of my body.

It was my first time relying on spiritual strength to get through a life threatening situation. I was about 15 years old when I visited Lake Champion for the second and last time. What I learned from that experience is that prayer works. It's a true saying that there are no atheists in fox holes because once I left summer camp at Lake Champion and returned to the group home, I became quite prayerful.

However, I stopped going to church by the time I turned 16. I didn't take an interest in Christianity again until I joined the gospel choir in college. But that didn't work out for me for too long either. Yet it was in college where I did the most research on religion, its history and origins. I wanted to know if religion was man-made or true Divinity. I learned that the first monotheistic spiritual system was introduced by Black Africans more than 2500 years ago and influenced almost all of the religious belief systems of today therefore, religions are man-made and woman-made paradigms. Throughout history, there have always been people who believe that God is a woman.

My favorite spiritual teachers are mystics like: Muata Ashby, Osho, Mother Theresa, the Dalai Lama, Thich Nhat Hanh and the poet Rumi. They provide timeless wisdom that I can always return to. Through Zen Buddhist teachings, I learned the art of meditation. Ironically, learning to meditate came to me at a time in my life when I was atheist, around the time I graduated from college. Buddhism seemed to be the most logical way to practice spirituality but there was no God, as I knew it, in Buddhism. As a practicing Bodhisatta, I became a vegetarian, practiced meditation and threw my television away so that I could become less attached to stuff and more mindful to life. I used Taoist koans as a source of inspiration for many lengthy meditations. Eventually, meditation reconnected me with God - but it wasn't the Zen style of meditation that brought me all the way home.

I would make the shift from dogmatically practicing Zen Buddhism to simply being aware of my spiritual nature just a few years later when I was invited by a male friend, Sekhmet, to a Native American style, full moon meditation ceremony. Pursuing spirituality through the consumption of hallucinogenic, plant based, teas gave me a clearer understanding than any of my previous experiences or research.

The person who invited me to the full moon meditation, Sekhmet, was someone that I confided in. He knew that I was heartbroken after breaking off an engagement and the relationship that I thought would last forever. I was still in my twenties where idealism reigned supreme. Yet, I had been strong enough to end that relationship once I confirmed that my potential husband was a cheater.

I did not believe in God, I did not have family to emotionally support me, being in that relationship and living with my fiancé for over 2 years I had lost touch with my close girlfriends and could not just call them up all of a sudden for emotional support now that my romantic relationship was over.

So when my friend Sekhmet urgently referred me to a meditation I knew it was because he could sense the heaviness of my heart and the emptiness of my spirit. I took his referral very seriously as he highly recommended it saying that he had just done it the night before. He said that "this" meditation changed his life for the better and had impacted his whole way of thinking. His story was inspiring and gave me interest in experiencing it. After all, I was no stranger to meditation. It also didn't hurt that Sekhmet was a fashion model, personal trainer and well-informed health nut. I wanted to believe him.

I called the meditation facilitator to make an appointment immediately. The facilitator, a Native American named Sunset, said that I sounded like I needed to do a meditation, like yesterday. He gave me an appointment to come to a small group meditation that night even though he had just facilitated a meditation the night before. I was flattered that he was so generous and willing to help me right away. The location was just half a mile away, I could walk there. He told me to bring some flowers but I knew that between his house and mine there would be no place to buy flowers. Instead, I bought some mangoes and half of a watermelon along the way as an offering in place of the flowers.

I had no idea what I was getting myself into. I was emotionally devastated and experiencing some really negative emotions following a broken relationship so I wanted help ASAP but did not know where to turn. Around 6:00 PM I met Sunset at his Spiritual center which was set up with pyramids in every ceiling corner of the room as well as a larger pyramid hanging from the center of the ceiling, over our heads. He had a huge waterfall which you could hear constantly running in the background. I felt at peace with the total arrangement.

We talked for a while about what brought me to this meditation including all the emotional stress I was under from just coming out of a relationship and from the way that I was, or rather *was not*, raised in foster care. Eventually, a couple came and Sunset said that we had been waiting on their arrival to begin the Prayer Circle (he called it that).

The couple that showed up was awesomely beautiful. They appeared to be extremely healthy, with glowing skin and yoga master, toned bodies. One could tell that they were holistic in their diet and that they worked out. At the oldest, they appeared to be in their thirties although it was later revealed that they each had adult children who were at the age that I had mistaken them for being. They were African-Americans with dreadlocks, like mine, that were well maintained. I felt that they were outstanding role models and a good example for the African-American community especially because they were together as an equally yoked couple. I was impressed by their individual images and combined image. I wished they were my parents.

Sunset introduced me to the couple, Maureen and her man Mojo, and we made small talk. Both members of the couple said they wanted to use the meditation as a tool to heal their relationships with their offspring. I opened up to them and told them the major issues I wanted to address: I had just broken off an engagement and had grown up in foster care. They offered me sympathy and I refused it saying that I was there to work through it. I had a sincere desire to confront my problems in their entirety and analyze them until they became rational to me, less emotional and less scary. I no longer wanted to be a prisoner to my memories. I did however want to take control of my being, mentally and physically. I wanted to repair myself from the inside out.

The facilitator, Sunset, started the prayer circle by having us join hands and chant: OM and HU. We each took turns inviting our ancestors, angels and ascended masters to join us in our journey. He turned on some speakers that played a mix of Native American flute music and Hare Krishna chant music. Then he gave us some herbal teas to drink. The first cup of tea smelled and tasted like burnt, bitter, black coffee without sugar. The second cup of tea had a pretty fuchsia color to it and it didn't smell bad but it was the driest liquid that I have ever swallowed in my life. After I drank it my mouth felt dry like chalk. The sensation that the teas gave me was like a warm wave coming over me.

We all spread out on the floor on yoga mats with blankets. Sunset was going to watch over us, Maureen and Mojo were meditating as individuals in separate corners of the room. I started to notice the huge plants on the window sills. Candles were lit up in the room on top of bookcases so they were positioned at a safe height, about a foot from the ceiling. We were all sitting on the floor, just quietly looking around when suddenly I saw the candle flames jumping from one candle to another. And every time I looked back and forth to confirm whether the flames were actually jumping or if my vision was just blurry, the number of flames that I saw increased and started flashing from one end of the room to the next with increasing speed. Every time I blinked the number of lights increased. So I asked Sunset and the other two participants "Why am I seeing all these lights, am I high or something?"

They were talking but they weren't quite answering me so I kept asking the same question over and over again. Sunset finally said "You are not high. You are seeing a glimpse of the light that is inside of you. You are like the lion that goes around saying 'baaa, I'm a sheep, baaa' until someone shows it his reflection in the mirror and he realizes that he is a lion."

All 4 of us simultaneously burst out laughing at the thought of a lion "baaaing" like a sheep. We continued talking to each other from our individual yoga mats and as we started getting into the realm of meditation the conversations drifted off and on.

I closed my eyes and saw a myriad of colors, so I kept popping my eyes back open to make sure that I wasn't going crazy. Interacting with the other participants kept me in touch with my sanity. I felt extremely nauseous and desperately wanted to throw up just to feel relief. About an hour or two after initiating the meditation, I actually threw up. Each of us was provided with a plastic bag in which to vomit so I did not feel embarrassed about it. Sunset came to my side and told me to ask my spirit what was coming up via vomiting and if it needed to be released. It was then that spirit told me that my vomit was symbolic of negative energy coming out.

After my stomach was emptied out, I laid back down and closed my eyes. My spirit showed me my dirty deeds. It was like my entire lifetime, specifically edited to feature all of my wrongdoings was flashing before my eyes. I felt very ashamed of myself to the extent that I began crying hard but quietly because there were others in the room. I cried for a couple of hours. My nasal passages were blocked and clogged due to the congestion from crying. I was rocking my body back and forth holding my arms around myself like I was hugging and holding myself or trying to comfort myself. Maureen kept rising to hug me every hour or so, Sunset performed reflexology on my feet and the Mojo kept asking me for permission to communicate with me.

In the middle of it all, we all sat up at the same time and started talking to each other. Out of nowhere Maureen says "I have a taste for some..." then she and Sunset said simultaneously "Watermelon!" Maureen had no way of knowing that I had brought watermelon (and enough to share with 4 adults, mind you) as an offering to the mediation because I was supposed to bring flowers instead and I had gotten there before her. This was a purely synergistic moment.

Sunset left us in the room to go cut up the watermelon that I had brought. It was such an interesting phenomenon because Maureen did not know that watermelon was available to be had, she just made a statement. And it boosted my meditation knowing that there was fruit for us to eat, that we were on the same wavelength and that I had the foresight to bring enough watermelon for all of us despite the fact that I had planned on doing the meditation alone. We ate that watermelon like it was the last on earth and we each commented on how gratifying it was. Then we resumed the meditation.

Off and on Mojo would make conversation with me and I would sit up. I would be sniffling and still crying somewhat uncontrollably but I would talk to the others as if nothing was wrong because I was crying for many different reasons in my meditation that had nothing to do with the real, physical world. My consciousness was bouncing back and forth from the physical to the spiritual realms. Interestingly, my crying was a physical behavior that I was almost unaware of because in my meditative phases, I was going through mood swings from blissful happiness to sadness and sorrow and back to blissful happiness. The depth of emotion I was experiencing was causing me to cry as there are tears of joy and tears of sorrow.

I'm guessing that around midnight an Afro-Caribbean Band and started beating drums outside in the streets. It was the Eastern Parkway *Juve'*. It happens the night before Brooklyn's annual Labor Day Parade. At the moment, it was raising my spiritual energy. The sound of the drums boosted my meditation and I was really beginning to feel the spiritual energy in a much more profound way.

I got to a point in my meditation that was like running through a forest with leaves crunching under my feet. During the daylight hours, I am guessing around 5:00 AM or 6:00 AM, Sunset gave me a rose quartz crystal. He said he had been guided to give it to me by his spirit. He told me to hold it close to my heart as it is a heart healer. It was a perfectly round, smooth, cold marble feeling crystal that was pink with milky white color in it.

At this point in time my meditation was beginning to fade off but when I placed that crystal in my hand and over my heart, I felt a surge of loving energy shoot through my heart and outward throughout my whole body, like a warm vibration. I know what it's like to get goose bumps on the outside of my skin. But this sensation was like getting goose bumps on the inside, under my skin. It was comparable to dropping a stone in a still body of water, there was a rippling of chi energy flowing throughout my whole body. I curled up with the rose quartz crystal into a fetal position and just felt the positive vibrations until I drifted off into sleep.

We all arose sometime between 9:00 AM and 10:00 AM. We talked about our experiences. Mojo said that he saw light emanating from me that was tremendous and that he saw angels making love on the ceiling. He said that he felt blissful love coming from me and that it filled them with joy. He also said that he communicated with his ancient Egyptian ancestors. I told Maureen and Mojo that I considered them to be my spiritual parents and the facilitator, Sunset, to be my Doctor because I had died and been reborn over the course of our night together. I told them that I had shed a lot of negative habits and tendencies and that now I felt whole.

I explained how the combination of their presence, the *Juve'* music and Sunset's support helped facilitate my transition from the old me to the new me and it was nothing short of my spiritual rebirthing. I told them that the spirit told me that I had already lived a lifetime in my 23 years and it was time to die and be reborn again. I told them that I was a different person now and that I did not know how I would relate to my friends in my family from then on. They assured me it would be a natural and easy transition after all because I was a *better* person now. Sunset, Mojo, and Maureen thanked me for sharing positive energy with them and they expressed how proud they were that I had shed layers of adversities virtually overnight. Each of them had words of praise and kindness for me and I wished that we could have stayed there and talked for days. But we had to part. From 6:00 PM the night before until 2:00 PM the next day we had been at Sunset's place.

On the walk home, I got mixed up in the crowd of at least half a million Labor Day Parade spectators. It was drizzling very lightly outside and it felt perfect falling on my skin. I felt alive, lighthearted and free. The festive atmosphere perked me up even more and when I got home the air smelled pure in my apartment. It was a new day, the first day in my new life and it was beautiful.

Chapter 4: Divine Intervention

I can tell you what I saw in my meditation when my eyes were closed and I was not distracted by the environment. My prayer circle experience was totally based on trust and to this day I have no knowledge of exactly what I consumed in those herbal teas. I will share my inner experience with you for the sake of scientific research. I am not promoting the use or abuse of any mind altering substances. But since it was a spiritual trip, I don't mind sharing the visions I had within a state of deep meditation:

I saw myself flying up real high, like an escaped slave heading for heaven, with my arms at my sides and my head pointing upward toward the clouds. I thought that I wanted to sit on the clouds and roll around on them and just sit there for a while but tremendous feelings were coming over me, like emotional sensations and physical vibrations that I was in for much more than the clouds could offer and who was more deserving than I to have a unique experience?

Then I saw that I had an umbrella carrying me up with the effect of a hot air balloon. There was a child holding my hand that I must have picked up before leaving Earth. While ascending, I let go of the child's hand and it transformed into a spirit with wings and flew away like a wild firecracker. Somehow I knew that it would be safe to let go of the child in midair. I flew up and up and up until I saw a rainbow, I stood so close to the rainbow and was just suspended there right above it and just behind it but it would appear to anyone standing on earth that I was standing on top of the rainbow.

There were people standing on Earth way below me they seemed to be gathered on the grass like they were expecting an event or just came to enjoy the nice weather, but not necessarily paying any attention to me. I felt so good to have the opportunity to feel the rainbow radiating a multi-dimensional light and to be a part of it, so close to it. Just when I thought that it was the best ever feeling I could have, I began ascending again further up into the atmosphere. Finally, I was headed further up towards the clouds again which was where I really wanted to go and when I got there it was all that I thought it would be.

The clouds felt soft and firm, open to letting me float through them and supported me when I paused to rest on them. They felt like pillows but softer and without any resistance, like a soft blanket. After that experience, I began to ascend even higher unaware of where I was going until I saw that I was leaving Earth for outer space.

When I got there it was so empty and vast, so dark save for the stars. I did not see any planets only darkness and stars, then I started looking around wondering if it was worth floating or flying around because I thought it would look to same all over wherever I went out there. I did not know what to do or where to go next or why I was there or what was next... Then I saw the sun, it was brilliant and bright but not overpowering and while I stared at it, a stenciled outline of a smiling sun with rays passed over the actual sun like an eclipse and it created a rainbow of color as the genuine sunlight filled the stencil making it look alive and like it was smiling at me. Then I looked around into the darkness all around me.

Something starting happening to me that was totally uncontrolled by me. I'd transformed into a golden topaz, shaped like an elongated octagon, like a rectangle with the sides slanted off instead of squared off so it created an additional four sides to the rectangle. It took me a minute to realize that I was the gem, the topaz that I was seeing. It was my birth stone. Then the topaz began to open up like a pyramid pointing outward, it slowly opened up and a great sunlight poured forth with such power and awe and beauty and strength and force. It was incredible, awesome, huge, bright and totally amazing!

Words can't describe the feeling I get just thinking about it, the magnitude of the light shining in outer space surrounded by darkness, piercing the darkness, at one with the darkness, showing itself to me as I watched from a distance, for this light was tremendous and at the same time I was coming to the realization that this light was me, the gem was me, showing me what was inside of me. I was later told by Sunset that the outer space I saw was really inner space.

After I experienced the light, I remained in outer space and went back to a human form. I saw my human self suspended in air. I started to ask questions about what I needed to do to get my life together. A circular wheel spun around me, outside of me, with me in the center of it and right over my head it stopped with an image of my mother's face perfectly centered above my head and I knew that it meant that I must put her first. I was watching from a distance and actually, physically experiencing everything simultaneously. After coming to new conclusions about my mother and the fact that I must visit her, my father's image was brought up next, though not as vividly as my mother and I thought that I should call him and tell him that he had been doing a good job lately, being there for me and my brothers over the past two years.

Then I thought about my brothers and how I needed them to be there for me and I thought to call them and invite them over to visit me. I saw my father's image take its place next to my mother's above my head. Then I saw my father, my brothers and I sitting around a dinner table talking and holding hands like a truly connected family. And then I knew that I had to put my family first in order to get right with myself.

I started to do the real soul searching by asking questions about my life and identifying the problems. While in space I asked why my mother has had to suffer, why I had to suffer, why my boyfriend had to cheat on me, what I should be doing with my time and with my life, what my purpose is and how to fulfill on my destiny and why there is so much suffering in the world...

The spirit told me that there was no other way; there was no other way for me to come into divine consciousness and awareness that I am divine. There was no other way for me to become aware of my own divinity. That I was made perfect and in god's image; the suffering of the world is a necessity for God's work to be done through humanity. The pain and suffering I have experienced from childhood on through my recently failed relationship was all prerequisite to me learning to love myself and to nurture the God within and to feel as one with the people without, the people of the world. Each of us is divine and made perfect in God's image and each of us has

God within. The spirit is eternal and the flesh is temporary.

The feeling of flying high and floating in space was making me nauseous and I felt the need to purge. This is when I vomited (in real life people, not in my mind) and the facilitator told me to ask the spirit what was coming up out of me and the spirit told me that it was negative energy. I had only a handful of food to eat that morning and that was only chickpeas and collard greens. I had not eaten since around noon yet 10 or 12 hours later I was vomiting like I had just feasted. The thought of negativity coming out of me as I vomited forced my descent from the heavens in my meditation and I found myself in the street in front of a place I used to live where the landlord dabbled in the dark side of magic. I must have been equating him with evil, but this was not about him in the least.

I continued descending through and below the concrete, underground, down past the sewer, lower on down past the underground pipes, and even lower into the darkness where I came to terms with my own bad deeds.

All of the harmful words and actions I had taken against other people, all the accusations and judgments made, all the hurt and pain inflicted on others by myself and I knew that those things were misplaced anger and I felt guilty about the mean spirited things I had said to others. Now I said to myself: *if I want to be loved and forgiven after the things that I have done then why not love and forgive them to whom I have said and done things that were wrong?*

All I could feel was compassion, love and forgiveness for all the people who had done wrong to me. I wanted to call them and thank them for giving me a life experience that brought about the divine awareness I was witnessing and receiving as a blessing. Then I broke down emotionally and just became vulnerable to every bad feeling I've ever had. I was sorry for hurting others and for saying the things that I had said and doing all the terrible things that I had done. I began to search my memory for people to apologize to. I felt sorry for all the people I had hurt and had a great desire to call them and apologize. I broke down to the point of saying that I was just like a drop of rain, one of billions of people. God was everything.

While thinking that I was nothing I saw the suffering people of the world and felt the sufferings that they were experiencing. I stretched my hands out and was being followed and surrounded by the masses of people who were reaching out to me to receive the love I was pouring out. They were reaching out to me grabbing my hand and trying to touch me. They were running alongside me trying to keep me within view and within reach. I felt so much unconditional love for them.

Physically, in the real world, I was crying like a baby rolling around on my yoga mat, unable to breathe due to the congestion of having been crying for what seemed like hours. But spiritually, I was in heaven begging God to help me heal the hurt of the world. I asked God why there was so much pain in the world. God told me that it must be in order for divine awareness to happen. And I took that answer very personally, relating it to my own pain and suffering from childhood coming up in Foster Care, abandoned by my own drug addicted parents. Why did I have to bear so much pain from childhood through the present?

I saw my version of Jesus Christ and understood that my suffering was necessary in order for others not to suffer, that I must tell others to stop suffering. I felt like a female Jesus, God's chosen warrior and I felt blessed to be chosen. The spirit told me to go forth as a healer, emerge from my meditation as a healer of myself, a healer of nations, and a healer of my people. The spirit told me to judge not but to love unconditionally. The spirit told me that my pain and suffering were necessary in order for me to come into divine awareness and that it was the only way I could have received the blessings that were pouring out all over me and that had I not suffered I would not have been led to the divine awareness I was experiencing.

There was no other way. Had my parents not abandoned me as a four year old child, I would not have known that the pain of others could be so deep. Had my boyfriend not cheated on me I would not have been able to really let go of him emotionally and get to know myself. There was no other way that I was going to leave him for myself. I was holding onto worldly things without considering the burden and placed on my spirit. In the meditation, my (ex- fiancé) boyfriend was the hardest thing to let go of. In the real world he had begged me to stay with him and work things out. I had put him out of our apartment but I was having second thoughts about reuniting with him as I was still somewhat in love.

The meditation empowered me to suddenly let go of all the hurt and pain of years of abuse, maltreatment and neglect from Foster Care, I mentally forgave, apologized to and thanked the woman my fiancé had slept with. I was willing to let go of my possessions, cash and clothing. However, I was stuck on him, this man made of flesh. I had passed the point in my meditation where I learned that the flesh was meaningless. Yet I requested that the spirit allow me to hold onto **this** man. And after many spiritual "No's" I finally let go of him with the knowledge, wisdom and understanding that I was first. I was number one, there was only me and my oneness with me was essential to my oneness with God. God was inside of me and so was the light, sunlight, rainbows, angels and ancestors.

And then I knew that was the truth, I also knew that the divine awareness I was experiencing was knowledge of self, self- love and self- preservation. I knew that I was forgiving and being forgiven at the same time and I realize that the more I could let go of the pain and drama, the higher I could fly. I began to confront all of my fears. I realized that if I could accept the sufferings as a temporary state of the flesh that I could use my inner spirit to take me out of this world and allow me to fly again. I let go of every desire that I had to control, to judge others and make criticisms. I let go of all the criticisms I made of myself and boy did I fly!

When I say that I flew, in the spiritual sense, I mean it. I transformed into a pure spirit without the need for wings to fly. I was so liberated, so free, so happy to be me, light as a feather and 100% happy. When I had let go of everything that seemed so important I came to the conclusion that I am divine. I am beautiful. I am one with God, I am one with nature. It hit me that I was everything. I was every man, woman and child. I had power from being perfectly crafted in God's image. I was unconditionally loved because the most high lived in me as part of me and was always with me. I realized that I was not alone, God has my back at all times, guiding and loving me. I had to let go of all the hurt and pain in order to grow and that if all

I had was me - I was good enough. I learned to hold onto myself for comfort and to be happy with myself. I realized that I had been there for everyone else except for myself. I had looked everywhere else for answers but to myself. I had to learn to trust myself and to be all right with my decisions. Most of all, I have to be all right with myself.

As I came to terms with the notion of unconditional love for myself *and* others, I began to ascend towards the heavens again, this time I was riding up a platform without handlebars or anything but I was not afraid. It took awhile to completely ascend up out of the darkness and the ride was worth it because a myriad of colors were presented to me as I rode up. I was feeling divine and enjoying the spirit of God. I began to thank God over and over again. When I was done with that I began to thank all the people that had impacted my life positively or negatively over and over again. I thanked God for showering me with much needed love and I was shocked that I had been so unaware of the existence of this magnificent love that was inside of me.

No one was pointing a finger at me telling me what to do, yet things work in divine order inside of me, what a divine revelation. As I ascended more the feelings of joy, peace and happiness overwhelmed me. I had nothing but love for myself and the world. I traveled all the way to heaven and met with the angels. I was surrounded by what looked like a paradise island and there were lots of angels. But still I felt that I had places to go and people to see on earth so I got ready to leave soon after getting there. An angel again asked me if I wanted to go or stay with them and I said that I wanted to return to earth and do some work because I was not ready to stay up there yet. The angels flew up and away.

I gathered myself, looked around and I saw that I was in a fairy tale looking forest. I was in the fetal sleeping position and it felt good to lie on this forest floor. I got up and walked barefoot feeling the leaves crunch under my feet and I felt like it was the best sensation that I had experienced with nature. I told myself that I loved the fall season, particularly the leaves crunching under my feet. I walked faster and faster feeling like a baby that was rapidly growing into a child and then morphing into an adult. I realized that I needed to grow up right then and there, so I did.

As I walked through the forest I knew that there was something out there for me to find so I walked faster and faster until I was practically jogging, then I began running cautiously, so as not to trip, but briskly so as to find what I was looking for quickly. The forest was beautiful shades of hunter green and burgundy and it was real dark. I could not see too much of head of me but I knew that I was safe and in divine arms so there was nothing that would hurt me out there and it gave me the courage to look harder and harder for the truth.

I had already asked all the questions on my mind and I thought the forest was a place to run around for fun after a while, but then I got restless and started to ask why I was there and what the lesson there was. The spirit responded immediately - *PATIENCE, you want everything now and you can have everything, just not right now.* And I agreed that I needed patience. The spirit introduced me to many lessons such as the need for greater productivity on my part and less selfishness in my dealings with others. The spirit also encouraged me to not feel bad about putting myself and taking better care of myself. The spirit told me that life should be enjoyed and that I should travel and enjoy myself. The spirit was so generously communicating with me and I could not see or perceive the source of this information. It was as if I were talking to myself but I'd never said these things before. The running I was doing was facilitating the pace at which I was receiving information. The faster and harder I tried to run in my meditation, the faster and more meaningful was the information that came to me.

I asked why I was there and I was told that I liked it there. It was beautiful but I had no idea that I liked forests (in this deep state of meditation, I did not recollect camping at Lake Champion as a teenager at all.) Then I asked what my purpose in life was and the spirit reminded me that my purpose was to heal myself and go forth as a healer. I wondered what that meant, heal, in what way? Then I saw myself on the pulpit, testifying, hollering and crying about the goodness of God and the fact that there was so much love inside of us, each of us and not just me. I saw myself trying to explain to the people that God was inside each of us and that each of us was divine if we could just stop looking toward the sky and begin to look inside.

Then I saw myself testifying in front of hundreds of people in church and I saw myself doing it over and over again at various churches like a guest preacher with a profound message. I had a burning desire to testify, not to be called by anyone but to go to church and testify. But then I thought *what if they don't want to hear about looking inside instead of looking outside?* And I thought the Church might be an ideal place to motivate people to find out that they were intrinsically divine. I saw myself motivating a large audience at a conference by telling them that we had a divine mission to manifest a positive destiny for ourselves and our children for the future. I saw the energy in the room rising and the people called out as if to agree and verbalize their unity with my proposal.

After I had testified enough, I returned to the forest and kept running, once again trying to figure out what my next question was. What else did I want to know or do? Travel, I've always wanted to travel far and wide. Immediately, I was transplanted to some of the most naturally preserved places on the planet. Very briefly I visited islands, countries and forests around the world, and I felt fulfilled like I had traveled the world without having to take a single step.

It was at this time during the daylight hours, I am guessing around 5:00 AM or 6:00 AM, that the facilitator Sunset gave me a rose quartz crystal. He said he had been guided to give it to me by his spirit. He told me to hold it close to my heart as it is a heart healer. It was a perfectly round, smooth, cold marble feeling crystal that was pink with milky white color in it. At this point in time my meditation was beginning to fade off. However, when I placed that crystal in my hand and over my heart, I felt a surge of loving energy shoot through my heart and outward throughout my whole body, like a warm vibration. I know what it's like to get goose bumps on the outside of my skin such as when I hear Whitney Houston's rich and powerful voice. But this sensation was like getting goose bumps on the inside, under my skin. It was comparable to dropping a stone in a still body of water, there was a rippling of chi energy flowing through my body. I curled up with the rose quartz crystal into a fetal position and just felt the positive vibrations until I drifted off into sleep.

Chapter 5: Reality Is Beautiful

Life after my first meditation became much more fluid. I started to shape my personality in a certain way that was more consistent with feminine ideals. For example, the "old me" - although good looking on the outside - was known by others to be confrontational, aggressive and energetically masculine. When I was in High School the Principal told me that I had too much testosterone. When I was 18 years old, my boyfriend told me that he felt emasculated when he was with me. From then on, men reported being intimidated by me. But now, as a result of this spiritually grounding meditation I was ready to humble myself and become vulnerable in such a way that other people could see it.

Every day I contemplated how I could become more feminine, more receptive. As a clothing designer, I would make myself long skirts and dresses that I felt comfortable and sexy wearing. But I needed to make a deeper shift. And so I prayed: *Dear God, please help me to become more vulnerable. I don't know how to do it myself and I can't afford to go to charm school so please, please, please show me how to show the real me. Is there some way that I can learn?*

I did not want to forget any of the things that I learned in the meditation at Sunset's facility so I had typed it out the day after. I made sure to print it and then store it in a 3 ring binder where I kept print outs of my astrology charts, numerology charts and Myers-Briggs Type Indicator results. I am a major self- help junkie, I know. But all of these personality tests and things were showing me that I was on the right path. The results of these self-inquiries showed me that I was on my path because the readings described me in a ways that were very consistent with my passions, interests, career and hobbies.

According to my astrological and numerological readings I was destined to be an artist, counselor and/or educator and that was exactly what my life was all about. But it wasn't enough. I wanted to be a better person – on the inside. And in that moment for me, being a better person meant giving others an experience of me that made them feel comfortable when they were *with* me. I wouldn't know that I had become a better person until other people could experience it and say "wow, you are much cooler now than you used to be." My early twenties had been filled with self-doubt and second guessing myself. For the first time, I did not require confirmation from another person to know what I should do next.

At this point, I was two years post-college, into my career. I earned a Bachelor's Degree in Psychology and got my first full-time job with a salary and benefits. Initially, I was hired to be a Counselor in a public shelter, but I was quickly promoted into the Training and Education Department. My job was to facilitate Adult Basic Education workshops and make employment referrals to the residents. Looking back, my greatest accomplishment was being acknowledged by the agency's Director in a letter of praise which stated that I had exceeded the numbers met by the other NYC shelters for training and employment placements and retentions. After three successful years on the job, I decided to find another job in order to make higher pay.

My next job was being the Substance Abuse Counselor for a medical facility that serviced terminally ill patients. My entire caseload consisted of dying patients. I would get a negative reaction from people when I used to tell them that I worked at a public shelter in NYC. But now, even my own mother did not approve of the fact that I worked strictly with people who were sickly.

It sounds worse than it really was. You see, working with this population was my best professional experience. My patients were truly amazing. The *only* problem was that sometimes they died. It would leave a gap in my heart. Other than that it was my favorite job. I was hired to monitor the progress of people who had a history of substance abuse and/or mental illness but were now stabilized due to their illness. When I went to their homes I would inspect for cleanliness, food supply and make sure that they were generally feeling well.

The main reason this was my favorite job was that the patients were always so kind, upbeat and positive. You would never suspect that they were ill. Sometimes the patients would come into the office and visit my cubicle wearing the biggest, brightest smiles on their faces. It seemed like the diagnosis gave them a new lease on life as opposed to taking it away from them. I never had an angry or hostile patient. Occasionally I would run into patients on the subway in NYC and they would maintain a high level of professional respect for me. I really appreciated that because I was considerably younger than the patients.

But as much as I loved that job, it would be the first job that I'd get fired from. We worked in the basement of a residential building. On my day off work, a waste pipe burst in the ceiling over our office. When I returned to work the next day I was informed that my cubicle and the one next to it had gotten "wet" from this ceiling accident. The ceiling tiles above my co-workers desks had brown stained puddles in them but had not begun to leak yet. There had been no clean-up efforts made by the staff or maintenance workers and the office smelled damp and funky like old urine. A rumor was going around that it was a bathroom pipe that had burst over their heads.

What would you do? I did what I thought was the right thing to do. I asked the Director to have my cubicle cleaned especially the desk and computer and I requested a replacement chair, the fabric of my old seat was noticeably soiled. The Director listened to me but did not agree. I refused to work in that cubicle so I wrote an email from the secretary's desk to the Executive Director, who worked on another floor, asking him to intervene and have our office cleaned properly considering that the water stains were brown and really smelly. By the close of business, he had not responded.

The next morning, I returned to work and the stench of urine was really thick throughout the entire basement. To make matters even worse we had a few (terminally ill) patients coming in the office that morning for a health workshop. When the patients arrived, I left the basement and went upstairs to the Executive Director's office. I walked into his office and verbally explained to him that the pipes over our basement office had burst two days ago, there had been some leakage which now had a bad odor and now there were patients sitting around in this filth, breathing it in. I expressed my frustrations that the staff had to sit in those conditions as well. Then I asked him to schedule a clean up.

The Executive Director had a television in his office and as I spoke I glanced at it and noticed that he had been watching tennis before I barged in. *Did he even get my email from yesterday?* He paid attention while I spoke but when I was finished he said the he had already spoken to the Director of my unit about it and as far as they were concerned, I should clean my own cubicle.

I shouldn't have to clean up two-day old human waste from the waste pipe of a large residential building. But I did have to leave his plush office with the big sunlit windows all around it. I went back down to the basement where the patients were waiting. They had begun to talk amongst themselves about the stench and how bad it smelled. There were no windows down there so the patients had opened a side door to let fresh air in. I wanted to cancel the workshop, but it was not within my authority. I was concerned about the fact that the patients were not supposed to be subject to this type of air quality. I was concerned for my health and safety and for my co-workers' as well even though they remained silent.

No one was going to do anything about it so I picked up the phone and called the Occupational Safety and Health Administration (OSHA). I explained the situation and gave them the Executive Director's email address. Apparently he finally got my message because less than an hour later, the workshop was cancelled, the patients were sent home, the full staff was sent home and the office was closed for the rest of the week while a professional cleaning service came in to properly clean and disinfect the entire office. Even the floors were cleaned and repainted. Yes, the floors were painted.

The following week, when the office was cleaned out and re-opened, the Executive Director called me up to his office. He scolded me for calling an outside agency and said that he could not trust me anymore. I defended my actions as best as I could and I stood by our patients' rights as well. A few weeks later, I was fired. The termination letter stated that I had shown a lack of respect for the Executive Director.

I called Sunset as soon a s I got home and told him that I had gotten fired from my job. He just busted out laughing and said "Congratulations!" I wasn't amused. I started calling all of my friends to see if anyone could hook me up at their job by giving me a good reference. No one had any leads so I took a part-time temp assignment as a receptionist. It was better than nothing, but I was beyond bored working at a desk job where all I did was answer the phone lines.

As receptionists are prone to do, I found myself surfing the internet. It was far more entertaining to check my email accounts on different social networking sites than it was to sit around staring at the wall waiting for the phone to ring again. Social networking sites have their ways of pulling you in, one minute I was reading the latest celebrity gossip and the next minute one of my old college buddies named Jamal was instant messaging me about a fast upcoming trip to Brazil.

Jamal was a History major and member of the Muslim Student's Association in college when I met him. We used to sit around the cafeteria and talk for hours about religion, history and culture. It was no surprise to me that he had a big trip to Brazil planned. He had already shot a small documentary in Africa that I'd heard about. Now he wanted to shoot a documentary in the Brazilian *favelas* of Rio de Janeiro, which were third-world slums. He offered to discuss his travel plans with me over drinks at an upscale lounge in Union Square, Manhattan. I accepted his invitation and a couple of days later we were reunited.

Just like old times, we went right back to the way we used to: debating geo-politics for hours while sharing our opinions on everything under the sun. It was our way of having fun. I was beyond impressed with Jamal, he was really sharp, politically astute and he could converse on a global level. I was fascinated by the stories he told me about his travels to third world countries. He said that he planned to piece the footage from his travels together in order to create a humanitarian documentary that could potentially bring relief to impoverished areas.

After telling me a story in which he was kidnapped, detained and beaten for filming the bad conditions in a foreign country, he asked me to join the board of directors for his film company. I immediately declined. I've seen the series *"Locked Up Abroad"* on cable and let me tell you something: ain't nobody got time for that! So I basically told him "I don't know you well enough to go into business with you and I certainly don't know your crew members. Thanks but no thanks. Friendship doesn't mix with business anyway, you know that old saying."

He flashed a wide, toothy grin. He was a dark skinned brother with pearly white teeth. His charisma took over when he casually said to me "Why don't you come with us to Brazil?" I was flabbergasted but I did not show it, I recovered quickly: "Brazil? What language do they speak there *Spanish*? I can barely speak good English but seriously, when are you guys going?"

He just laughed and said "we are leaving in six weeks, so you have six whole weeks to get yourself a passport, a plane ticket and a Portuguese translation dictionary." I hadn't even said yes yet but how could I say no? The trip was only going to be eight days long, my temp assignment would end two weeks before the trip and I would be unemployed again anyway. Based on my internet research the exchange rate for one US dollar was three whole Brazilian dollars which sounded like a gold mine in a vacation to me.

I had been flying by myself from the age of fifteen to different states like Florida and Georgia to visit my biological family from time to time. I had been on vacation in Miami with my girlfriends before but I had never thought to travel outside of the United States. Regardless, I managed to pull myself together in the nick of time. I bought that ticket to Rio de Janeiro, then got an expedited passport, reserved a room in a hotel that was within walking distance of the world famous *Ipanema Beach* and at the very, very last minute I got a visa for my eight day stay . The next thing you know, I was on a sixteen hour flight to Brazil (I bought a less expensive ticket with a few layovers). I met Jamal and his crew at the airport in Rio de Janeiro where we had all landed around the same time. We actually wound up waving to each other from different positions on the customs line.

Jamal had three guys with him as his crew. After getting through customs, we grabbed our luggage from the baggage claim carousel and went to the money exchange center. We all shared a cab from the airport into the city of Rio and... Oh my goodness! Rio de Janeiro was everything that I had ever imagined, seen, heard or read.

The weather was like a summery dream, perfectly warm, sunny and breezy. Brazilian people were beautiful looking and sounding. It was all poetry in motion. Taking the city in visually while on the cab ride was totally uplifting to my spirit. If I looked to the right there was the beach, if I looked to the left it was a clean city with enough hustle and bustle to rival the energetic frequency of New York City. Looking straight ahead down the traffic road, it appeared that a few miles ahead, the cab could eventually drive us right into a mountain! Rio de Janeiro is a perfect city because it balances the seriousness of a gritty concrete city, with the playfulness of the beach and tops it off with a grounding energy from the green capped distant mountains in random places.

The cab driver's first stop was my hotel. I was dropped off first because Jamal wanted to know where I was staying. All 4 of the guys were going to stay in an upscale apartment rental one block away from the upscale *Copacabana Beach*, while my hotel was just about 5 blocks away from the general public/touristy but still world famous, *Ipanema* beach.

I gave him the business card to my hotel and Jamal gave me the phone number to his international cell phone. We quickly decided that in a few hours I would walk over to their hotel apartment where we'd all have dinner together then go club hopping for the rest of the night.

I settled into my hotel room quite easily even though the hotel staff spoke little to no English, I had a nice, big room but I needed to buy outlet converters in order to charge up my electrical devices. All of the television channels and radio stations were broadcasting in Portuguese which I have no knowledge of. I had accidentally left my Portuguese translation guide at home and would have to go out and buy a new one. After I showered and changed for dinner into a skimpy dress that would also look great on me at the clubs later on, I decided to start a journal, a daily log, before leaving my hotel room for the first time.

This was only an eight day trip but it was my first time leaving the USA and going to a place where I did not know the language. It's a good thing that I started a diary and photographic journal while in Brazil because as it turned out I would be on my own in this foreign country after just a few days. And I would gather the courage to extend my trip by an additional 20 more days. Not only did I stay in Brazil for a total of 28 days but I also flew out of Rio de Janeiro into Bahia for the middle portion of my trip. All in all, I went to Rio for about two weeks, then flew to Bahia for about ten days then flew back to Rio for a few more days before actually heading back to the USA. I was fearless, I was free and I was having fun. Too much fun, it could be said. By then end of my trip I found myself knee deep in trouble and in need of a miracle to get my arse back home safely.

Chapter 6: Lost On Vacation

The story of my 28 day stay in Brazil is better told through my journals because the story is told in real time and was written by me as a daily log in the middle to the end of each day as my trip was occurring. I have not omitted anything that would embarrass me, with the exception of people's real names. I wrote and kept this journal because I so loved everything Brazilian, that I did not want to forget ANYTHING! Please, don't judge me for what you are about to read but do prepare yourself for a wild ride through a hot, sexy and dangerous foreign country…

Day One

Arrived at hotel roughly 2pm, exchange rate at airport $3 Brazilian Dollars (Reals, Rs) to $1 US Dollar so $75 USD = $225 Rs. In other words, I'm rich here.

Hotel neat and clean, walk to beach 5 minutes away. Spent an hour or two in the hotel room paralyzed by fear of getting hurt, robbed or kidnapped as per people's warnings before I left.

Met Mina, a hotel neighbor who agreed to roll with me that night clubbing, stood me up when it was time to go.

I had seen Jamal in airport on line at customs, said he was going to a Copacabana hotel, I showered, dressed and walked to Jamal's hotel to familiarize myself with the neighborhood, beachfront and to meet people. Had dinner with Jamal and his crew, they talked about filming their sexual exploits. Silly of me to think they were here for anything other than sex tourism. Rather go to the club alone than with these nasty boys, after dinner, told them I was jet lagged and heading back to my hotel room to get some sleep.

Night One

Left my hotel room alone around midnight in hopes of clubbing, took taxi to a highly recommended area called "La Pa, Lapa"- crowded street festival- clubs- bars- restaurants. The entire community comes out at night. Met Rastas, was seduced by fine ass dude with dreads, tall, brown, muscular, shirtless, kissing and sucking my ear and neck while pulling my hair back as we slow danced. My booty bulging through a mini skirt, rubbing up and down on his fat, thick, long dick. He caressed my waist, thighs, hips and breasts while whispering Portuguese in my ear all the things he wanted to do to me.

Before him, I had met a few folks with dreadlocks here, like myself. I bought necklaces that represented the Orishas, walked around with a super cute dread Viktor who smoked weed with me and his friend, a white dread who sold t-shirts like an addidas logo look-a-like that was a weed plant and a red tee with yellow golden arches that looked like it said "McDonalds" but it really said "Marijuana." Anyway, my sexy dancing buddy was selling jewelry with the bootleg tee shirt dude and that's how I met him "Bobby." His shorts hung slightly exposing the crack of his ass, very sexy, he grabbed my hand after a few minutes of non-verbal communication, we couldn't understand each other anyway. Me- English. Him- native Brazilian Portuguese speaking.

He did clearly say "beautiful" in English and kissed me twice, I settled for it and leaned in for kisses on each cheek- customary Brazilian greeting, anyhow we danced in several clubs, always close. When we switched clubs he would walk ahead of me wriggling his fingers as if to say "hold my hand" and I gladly ran up behind him too cute in my kitten heels and mini skirt eying his tight muscular frame, long and lean, almond colored skin, sun blonded dread tips, thick lips, washboard stomach, beautiful smile. I would grab his hand because it was crowded, the kind of parade like crowding where you get easily separated, possibly lost from your friends. I was alone and other much less attractive men were trying to holler at a sister so I kept close to this muscular brother man.

He held my hand much different than it had ever been held before- his fore finger and thumb held my whole hand while his other fingers caressed the palm of my hand, we stopped to smoke weed a few times and in between doorways he asked me why I would smoke with but not kiss him, he would tuck my hand in the back of his pants as if to say "hold on." Did he know I was so seriously turned on by his ass? My fingers caressed it as we maneuvered through the crowd crack and all.

I told him "manana", thinking and meaning I would never see him again, damn I wished I had my camera for his fine ass, but I didn't want to be an obvious tourist whipping out my camera every five minutes. In a crowd this big, it could get lost or stolen anyways.

I saw the police chase and capture a man when I first arrived in Lapa by taxi. Not one out of hundreds or maybe thousands of people had a camera on them, I didn't even have a pocketbook, money in my bra. Anyway, he bought our beer, I asked him to buy me water, twice- he did, he bought me gum, my weed breath? Anyhow, he gave me his number, asked me to meet him the next morning (actually a few hours later) on Ipanema beach where he'd be selling his jewelry, he wore a ring he said he made from a sugar serving spoon and a bracelet he'd made from an actual fork, prongs holding a crystal in it- very chic. He wore a thick leather belt 3 or 4 inches wide with a piece of zebra skin on it- very chic with his sexy ass peeking out of sagging shorts.

Yeah, I considered fucking him royally but I declined, we shared a cab and split the cost of it 50/50 back to my hotel where I said goodbye like 3 times and that I'd see him in the morning which was a lie, he said posto 90 or 9? I said OK posto 90. Ipanema. It's a hang out spot on the beach.

Day Two

Morning, really afternoon, I woke about noon, ventured out about 1pm went in a different direction this time, smack dab into a street fair, good shit with "I know my worth" prices, I bought nothing, wanted everything, real thick leather furniture, clothing and accessories, crystals, endless artwork, I settled for snapshots, bumped into a girl I met at the NYC visa office, HEY! So good to speak English with a New Yorker, small world, no coincidences. Met her three friends said we were all headed to the beach and enjoying ourselves. I went to the beach alone, and walked as far out as possible, purchased rose quartz sphere on a silver stand for $30 Reals = $10US. I was happy though I really coveted a red, black green and gold Brazil windbreaker pants and Pele soccer Brazil Rio de Janeiro shirt, maybe Wednesday when my income tax comes in I can buy stuff, seeing but not purchasing put me in touch with my impulsiveness and later I realized that *I didn't need the stuff I would've bought on a whim if cash was on hand.*

I felt like an American brat, in other words- a jerk when I asked the clerk for a "normal American outlet to charge my cell." *Today I also got how beautiful I am* because Rio's women are world renown, yet Brazilian men, some of whom thought I was Brazilian were trying to holler at me. Went to the beach around 3pm, took pics of scene, saw fine ass brotha, giving me the eye, took pics of him, he took notice and was flattered, he was muscular as hell, jogging in white shorts, dreads pushed back.

He said "Hi"

I said "speak English?"

He stopped jogging and came over to me with a beautiful broad smile on his face. He said yes, his name was Sergio and he was from Angola living in Rio, already Portuguese speaking he said he spoke English too and he invited me to go see the movie "Million Dollar Baby" with him. I accepted, took another picture of him- he posed and smiled graciously, beautifully, I did not follow through on calling him for the movie. I turned my attention back to the beach and got present to a new reality, how rich the poor are, culture is everything, and materialism is nothing.

The poetry of the beach is: To be happy, friendly, and young at heart is to be rich, to be overweight and middle aged, while chilling in a bikini on the beach is to be rich. On the other hand, small children beg in the streets here. I went walking the endless "boardwalk" of Copacabana beach, countless vendors, entertainers and capoeiraists. I was looking for Bobby, the seductive dancer, after all.

After I'd walked like a mile or two it hit me after I asked for directions to post 9 or 90 as Bobby had instructed me, that I was on Copacabana beach, whilst Bobby said he'd be on Ipanema beach, the other tourists said I was 3 kilometers from where I wanted to be. I tried to walk not wanting to spend on a cab and when I got back to where I started, I felt like it was hopeless.

Then Jamal came up to me, took a random ass picture, out of nowhere, of me looking surprised to see him. He looked stupid in a Brazilian flag biker's du-rag and a bright ass yellow Brazil tee-shirt in cheap, make you sweat polyester fabric. After I made three or four jokes on his ridiculous "come-rob-me-I'm-an-American-tourist" outfit he took off the stupid hat and we started walking together. I told him I was tanning but was secretly disappointed to have given up my search for Bobby in place of lollygagging with Jamal.

Good thing is that Jamal invited me to tour with him in a cab to the favelas, waterfalls and the Jesus Christ statue atop a mountain where you'd get a 360 degree view of the Ipanema and Copacabana beach- of course I said yes. And it was his birthday, he invited me to go clubbing with him. So I went with him to his De-lux apartment in the sky- ninth floor condo in a time share building so he could get some more cash.

Beautiful, modern, 3 bedroom, 3 bathroom, parquet floor, magazine styled and furnished apartment with tasteful Brazilian art everywhere, DVD player, American English cable TV set up, leather couches, huge bedrooms and beds, etc. I was impressed, he said it was $1200 per week and he was splitting it with three others. "Oh", I said as I melted into the cold leather couch. My feet and legs were sore from walking two miles with a longing heart, in the wrong direction. Once again, I had given up hopes of seeing Bobby again.

We watched TV and talked some more. I agreed to go with him to HELP: a club/whorehouse, it was his birthday after all, we walked to my hotel room a few hours later so I could change, he bought me some KFC french fries, a salad and ice cream from McDonalds (the cleanest, safest looking and most affordable restaurants out there) I put on a mini-skirt and 2" heels, for dancing all night long.

I lied to Jamal and said I accidentally left my wallet at my hotel while we were in a cab on the way to the club. Truth is I was just low on cash and needed an ATM but really did not want to spend money in a club and felt that he as the horny jerk taking me to a sleazy, easy pick-up club, should at least buy my drinks. He caught my lie when I adjusted my bra to hide my money and he heard it crinkle and then we both knew that he'd busted me.

"You're buying me lunch tomorrow" is all that he said. I said "ok", and then whined "why?" "no reason," he said. At the club he said I was mistaken for his prostitute more than once (which was funny) by the waiter when he came back with Jamal's drinks (first water, then vodka, then a red bull). Jamal and I watched and laughed at the ho's and john's hooking up and negotiating before they separated or left together. Then I threw the booty on him and we danced dirty for an hour or two off and on. The music was very techno all night so we left the smoky stock exchange around 3am.

Day Three

We went back to his apartment where I spent the night in bed with him, but did not touch or seduce him. He was too immature to do anything besides playfully throw his arm and leg over me for a few minutes in the morning. We woke at roughly 10am. Their maid was preparing breakfast; Jamal offered me a fruit bowl of freshly cut watermelon, mango and papaya. I ate it then his three roommates came out. I tried not to look at them funny since minutes ago they let a prostitute out and an hour ago Jamal and I were awoken by the sounds of her moaning.

"Good Morning" the roommate said to me. "Good Morning" I said approaching them from the living room couch and taking a place at the table with Jamal and 3 roommates, all of us from NYC. We talked briefly about casual things until one of the roommates all but insisted that I have some of their cooked breakfast meal. Did they think that me and Jamal got it on the night before? I sure looked like it at that point, trying not to care.

Anyway, they were nice, pleasant guys and I wondered if American women who were more demanding caused average men like them to seek docile, sexy, foreign prostitutes. Jamal says some men pay for sex because they can't get it at home and the more they pay for sex, the lamer they are.

Jamal and I left for the beach where a cab driver was waiting to take us on a tour of the favela, waterfalls and the Christ statue. It was a good day, took lots of pictures and enjoyed the scenery. We didn't see the favela: driver said he'd take us tomorrow because police blocked the entrance. We got back round 5pm and walked around looking for my outlet converter, food and he needed a money gram- it was closed after all that walking! Anyway, I said I needed to charge my cell phone and iPod, so he offered me to come back to his spot and charge it. I went to my hotel to get my electronics then walked to his rental apartment, he wasn't there at the time he chastised me to be on time for, so I got upset and we had an argument after my things were charged about two hours later. I left and so did he- for the club HELP, again- said he didn't want to look bad in front of the guys though he really didn't want to go with them back to that club. Yea right. I took a cab back to my hotel.

Day Four

Got to Jamal's on time this morning, apparently he had a prostitute after all, his friends helped him get her out while I excused myself to the bathroom, Jamal didn't look me in the eye when he finally came out of the bedroom. I felt betrayed to an extent; I questioned myself- my ego? No, the pure hypocrisy I had argued with him about the night before. Lesson- I am learning over and over again- stay away from people that rub me the wrong way over and over again! Duh- why keep running into a brick wall? There is a reason you don't like them in the first place, it's called instinct, intuition. So why am I here, still writing? Because I want to go on a free tour, got nothing else to do and it's safer with someone else than with myself.

Got an email from the fabulous, handsome, sexy, gorgeous, photog, Ray from Brooklyn. He said he was going to the island of Bahia for three days either today or tomorrow. Bahia is a 2 hour plane ride from where I am in Rio. I wrote him back to have a good time because I am waiting for a money wire, hopefully tomorrow my money will be here from tax advance then I could get the hell out of here and really enjoy myself with Ray in Bahia. I will call my two friends Sergio and Bobby today or tonight, see what they're up to especially Sergio- he speaks English.

Jamal and I went to meet our tour guide, taxi driver, said we'd see the favela, downtown and Sugarloaf mountain top- we did. It took Jamal two hours to get money from the Money Gram before we went sight-seeing. The same cab driver takes us to and from everywhere. He asked me why I let Jamal go to the club "HELP" for the past two nights and if we were together. I got upset, offended and then I said "no we're not together, he slept with a prostitute." I told the cab driver how his roommates sat me in the dining room and when I went to the bathroom they let her out.

The cab driver told Jamal what I said, behind my back, when I got out to take a picture and when I came back Jamal was laughing like "we gotta talk, but not now because it'll ruin the day." I didn't know what he was talking about.

On top of Sugarloaf mountain (I took pictures) he outburst calling me names and throwing every negative thing he knew about me in my face. I told him he was a coward for waiting until we were on a mountain top when I had just told him the night before that I couldn't stand him and would not have him or someone like him as a lover. We cursed each other out all the way down in the cable car and then in the cab where I got exhausted telling him to shut the fuck up!

I wasn't embarrassed in front of the cab driver. It was his fault we were having this argument. I threw water in Jamal's face twice, and then whacked him in the head with my 1.5 liter plastic water bottle. He threatened to kill me but didn't touch me and I told him he was a weak ass punk. I held up my water bottle and reminded him that I bust him upside the head with it as I walked away drinking from the bottle. I hope I never see him again or somebody's going to Brazilian jail.

I called Sergio when I got back to my hotel; he said we could meet in an hour. We met an hour and a half later, good thing I was 15 minutes late, he was 30 minutes late (and is now 15 minutes late for our second meeting) but I was happy to see him and had just begun to worry that he wouldn't show up or had left my 15 minute late ass. Lesson- put myself first: I stopped to buy soap knowing it would make me late to meet him.

Anyhow, I was happy to see my Angolan/Brazilian black man dressed like a real New Yorker in a pink polo shirt, white NY Yankees hat, phat farm jeans and Tims. He looked great! I took a picture of him right away, secretly thanking Jamal in my mind for pushing me into SERGIO's arms. We hugged I think, then sat and talked.

I needed to use the bathroom so we went across the street to a Chinese restaurant where I spent $40R on delicious corn soup, vegetable fried rice and Chinese cabbage. He asked me if I had enough money, I said yes, knowing I couldn't afford it but paid anyway. I shared the food with him on the beach front hoping he'd be impressed by my generosity. We laughed and talked, he walked me home because I got cold on the beachfront. I told him about my day sightseeing, he said he'd take me to the club Thursday night and to Lapa again on Friday night when it was best and most crowded, more crowded than before?- Ohmygod!

He said he wanted to see me again, the next day. I told him I wanted to rent a bike, go places I had not been yet and see more of Rio. He said he had a bike and would show me Ipanema beach and posto 9, we laughed. He hugged me at my hotel gate, kissed me on the cheek and we planned to call each other the next day.

Day Five

Sergio called me as I was in the corridor eating apples for breakfast. I was pleased to hear from him, he told me to find a bike rental place and call him at 1pm. We met at posto 5 at about 1:45pm. He had a bike, I rented one. Off we went talking about everything. We knew the same things about the diasporic world of Africans/Black Americans and the expectations of us.

We saw Ipanema, I took pictures, and there was a hidden beach for the rich separated by like 50 feet at most of rock- a low mountain. We took a ride out into the rich people's neighborhood where he bought a smoothie of his favorite exotic fruit. I didn't like it so he offered to buy me another one. The night before he'd bought me a little light for my key chain that said "I Love You" in English. He was impressed when I told the salesman "obrigado" ("thank you" in Portuguese.) The salesman generously gave me like 4 or 5 extra batteries for the lighting effect and showed me how to turn it off and on. I was most grateful and so was the salesman, it was a beautiful moment of love, generosity and gratitude among three humbled people. My heart beat deeply as I experienced the moment with profound satisfaction. It was indeed very special to me.

I hope to retain the perfection of this moment in my heart's palpitations, my mind's eye and my brain's memory. It was a moment I could long for, be overwhelmed by and cry for, a highlight of my trip.

Lesson- Moments are riches, I am most grateful for the capacity to experience them on such a spiritual level and physical/mental level that was last night after dinner.

Today we met, rode bikes, I declined his offer to buy me a smoothie. I had drunk at least 8 cups of water and went to the bathroom at least 3 times to his amusement, we talked for a while about all kinds of music, and we listen to the same stuff. I took pics of him and had others take pics of us. We joked about me being a tourist with my camera out every five minutes for every little thing. He warned me to have rolls of film on my person through the airport or x-ray machines would destroy my images. I said I would have the pics developed here instead of back home.

He rode with me back through Ipanema beach and we walked into a cove with rocks and a beautiful view where he took pics of me. He showed me graffiti in a park that was awesome and he asked about the state of graffiti in New York. I told him it was on the decline because it was too much trouble to get into in NYC, he was disappointed but understood. I returned the bike late, Sergio negotiated with the guy to not charge me for the lateness then he said he had to go but wanted to see me later. I told him that I needed 2 hours to myself to check the internet, eat dinner, and would be back at my hotel before it got dark outside. He said he'd call and see me later and if not I could call him. He didn't call. I wanted to call him but wasn't able to from the hotel phones because he had a cell phone number that I couldn't figure out how to properly dial. The error messages were spoken in Portuguese.

I was exhausted and needed to sleep anyway. But I was looking forward to seeing him. I told him I found a health food store "Verde Mundo" which sold lemon pie that I wanted to taste. He said he would buy it and bring it to me- how sweet, however, in divine order we didn't connect tonight. Hopefully, tomorrow night we go to the club he promised.

I will call Bobby tomorrow, maybe finally put on a bikini and meet Bobby at Posto 9, smoke weed and take pics. On my walk, I went back to Verde

Mundo and bought 2 pendulums and a slice of the lemon meringue pie. It wasn't as good as it looked. I bought the last piece and planned to tell Sergio to get me the chocolate piece if/when we spoke tonight.

Lesson- Be grateful, don't have a false sense of entitlement, it feels good to be generous gracious and in gratitude. I got that yesterday.

Day Six

I'm up after 12am. Pendulum told me not to take that afternoon nap. I did anyway, now I am up with a rambling mind, restless, curious to know what time it is, training myself to let go of time, at least while on vacation because it doesn't matter and will create a false sense of urgency, to go to sleep, to wake up, to go outside, to do things, to be places. None of which really matters. Time makes you feel stressed about being active, how stupid.

So I am lucid and smiling, holding a huge, beautiful, round, rose quartz. I realized that I had apples for breakfast, avocados and raw veggie salad for lunch and then refined, fried, processed foods for dinner, because I feel hungrier cravings at night. Perhaps it's because the vibration of night is lower due to the sun being down that makes my will weaker?

Lesson- Shakti was right about processing feelings, things takes time to settle and process Be within the experience, you can't fully define what you're thinking or feeling until it passes. The past is easier to verbalize, interpret and communicate than the present.

Woke up and hit the beach roughly 12-2pm. Got a tan, sporting my bikini and had someone taking pics of me in it. Called Sergio and checked my bank account. Check deposited - not cleared though. Sergio and I agreed to meet at 6pm. I wanted to do laundry and have lunch. I got a soy patty and a veggie patty with tomatoes and eggplant in it, the soy patty had soy cheese in it too. They were both good. I had cold green tea and chocolate cream pie that was delicious like a mousse.

The laundry mat charged per load to wash and dry, 17 reals = roughly $6US. I can wait for more money to become available before doing laundry. I went back to the hotel courtyard and read my book about the ancient African path to immortality. Twice I got scared because first a group of boys, then a group of men acted like they were trying to break in the gate that separated us. I was behind the gate- alone. I had my camera and my wallet was in my pocketbook, credit and bank cards included, both groups kissed at and talked to me through the gate in Portuguese. I ignored them, both groups eventually went away after trying the gate. I wished to have taken pics of them but knew it would have been dumb and dangerous.

Went to the beach. Sergio was late again, I sat on the beach and watched a sexy fut-volley game: like volley ball played with a soccer ball, hit over a volley net, but no hands allowed. An OOOOOLD ass white man came over and sat at my table, "Congratulations" he said "you dressed yourself so well today, I've never seen toe rings before and two on each foot!"

I pretended like I did not speak English, "Nobrigad" ("No thanks" in Portuguese.)

Sergio popped up and kissed me on the forehead. We left Copacabana Beach for the cove in Ipanema Beach. I took a picture of his fine ass. He was holding a bag, I was tempted to say "What did you buy me?" but I didn't. He took pics of me in front of graffiti and climbing rocks and again sitting atop a rock with a view of Ipanema beach behind me. He presented me with lemon cream tarts. He said he went to Verde Mundo but they were out (I know) so he got his favorite lemon tarts elsewhere. One was for me and one was for him. I was sooo flattered, I took a picture of him holding the bag and the tarts, he had taken a bite out of his already. It was delicious.

We politicked atop that rock for hours, then I whipped out my iPod and we listened to music. He said he liked everything I played and knew almost all the songs including U2's "It's a beautiful day." It was all so romantic, we had so much in common. We seemed to know what the other was thinking on all subject matters. He was so gracious, he got close as if he wanted to kiss but couldn't get the right moment, he had beautiful lips and an endearing smile. We left to get food. He had fresh cheese and tomato on bread like pita and I had a salad. We shared a plate of fries and a cup of sugar cane juice freshly squeezed. He walked me to my hotel at midnight, said it was too early to go to the club. He said he'd shower change and be back for me at 1:30am.

Day Seven

Sergio was only 5 minutes late this time. We walked to the club "Bunker." We danced to Gangstar and The Roots lesser known rap songs, real hip hop, while B-Boys battled doing real authentic old skool break dancing. I was impressed with their moves and dedication. I told Sergio that Brazilians were better preserving hip hop, graffiti and break dancing than New York City.

We went to another section of the Bunker where they played funk music. It was fast paced electronica over which they rap in Portuguese. Sergio said he didn't like it. We left at 4:30am. He walked me to my hotel and said he'd call me later in the day, perhaps go with me to Jardin Botanic.

He said my Portuguese was better than his English, we laughed, he told me to correct his English without delay. I advised him to read English books for perfect grammar. We kissed on the cheek a few times and hugged twice.

I showered and washed my smoked out hair. Woke up 10:30am, put on sun screen, checked emails, headed to the beach in bikini #2, had someone take pics of me in it. Drank coconut water, ate fruit salad, laid down to tan for 1 hour on each side.

Drank more coconut water and then ate the jelly inside of my coconut. Called Sergio. Sergio said he was dancing in a commercial for money and would be done in 2 hours. He said to call him because he wanted to see me. I asked if we would still go to Lapa, he said yeş! And we'd take the bus. I want to experience riding the public bus here in Rio. It looks like fun. They travel at the speed of light. People jump off at some stops. The bus driver will slow down but not actually come to a full stop so you have to literally jump off and hit the ground running.

He told me to buy a calling card and said that he wouldn't be available to go to Jardin Botanico, that I should go and have a good time. It was

2:30pm, I told him I went to the beach and tanned for 2 hours, I told him I went from yellow to brown to black. "Now I am black, you'll tell me later if I am right?" He laughed, he said he'd see me later, "kisses" he said.

I was flattered, we have good chemistry, obviously on the same wavelength and we are both left handed. Yesterday he told me he needed a New York contact. I wondered if he was using me to be the one, nothing wrong with helping a brother out, I thought.

I dreamt two or three nights ago that a Portuguese man was wooing me and I rejected him saying that he'd have to give me a diamond ring to be with me- but I said it with an arrogant laugh like he could never save up enough money to afford a ring for me, his face dropped, the rejection set into his facial features like a dark cloud approaching a sunny street, he said "I did buy you a ring, it's in my pocket with a card." He tapped his pocket and I knew that I was being a jerk, he turned and left so as not to further embarrass himself.

I was using him and it became clear to me that I never liked him and had set an "impossible" task before him to prolong my using him. I sat there (in the dream) confronting myself, I did not go after him though I felt immense sorrow and compassion for him, but I did not want him- the best thing I could do in that moment was let him go. When I woke up, I barely analyzed this dream, now days later, the impact is very realistic.

Considering my relationship to male relatives, friends and romantic partners, it's like: what have you done for me lately, and what can you do for me right now? Those are the bases of my moods and willingness to be compassionate or shall I say unwillingness. Several things could be at the root: the role of men in a historical context, black women's theory "I can do bad all by myself" or simple, plain egotistical, selfishness and manipulation. The easiest thing to do is to say I got this way of being from my mother. The hard part is how do I undo this way of being?

So far I am good to Sergio, I bought food for us and shared it with him. I wasn't turned off when he told me he was unemployed, I pay for myself when we go to clubs, I don't ask him for anything- his generosity is so profound, I think I am on to something here.

Lesson- generosity begets generosity. A mini-guitar salesman played and taught me to play the instrument, it was joyous. I took a picture of him because he sat and talked with me eventually giving me his number and inviting me to go out clubbing with him- after I declined his pitch. The conversation was very difficult, yet not strained.

Sergio and I are meeting at 10pm, heading for Lapa via bus at 12am. I wonder if he'll recognize me with my hair in Bantu knots. Sergio was late as usual, said he thought he told me 10:30, I was like *riiiiiight*! Still he looked good as usual and was my official tour guide. He sat with me and bought me a coconut to drink from though I told him I'd just had one. He had his coconut split into three pieces and shared the scooped pieces with me.

He told me his life story about leaving Angola- the land of no opportunity, after completing High School and coming to Brazil where he labored in construction, getting promoted to brick layer, earning higher pay until he saved enough to travel. Then he went to Canada where he soon became homeless, in the shelter, got on welfare, and then found work once he got to the Angolan section of town. He said he walked the street like a crazy person not being able to speak English and the Canadians were not even kind. He said he came back to Brazil after 2 years in Canada and worked construction, then McDonald's, got his picture on the wall within one month of working there- he said this with extreme pride and said he'd email me his employee of the month picture, he said he got promoted a few times before getting fired because his ID was borrowed, so he couldn't produce the ID they needed to make him a manager. He said he styled his hair in a twisted up afro, said it was beautiful and that he'd email me that picture too.

This hairstyle got him a job in a clothing store where he was promoted to manager. His story was funny and filled with integrity, not pride. I laughed through it and told him it reminded me of "Coming to America." He said "I like my story" and he laughed.

I told him my story wasn't as funny but I had to pee first, he laughed, I peed like 50 times per day from drinking loads of water. It was an ongoing joke between us. We boarded the bus, Sergio paid for me. There was a turnstile you went through, it was big and red. The ride was comparable to a rollercoaster, complete with handles atop every seat ahead of you to hold on to. I gripped it with both hands! The buses speed, the roads are uneven, it's a fun ride though.

I told him my story, it was short and sweet. He knew I had been a counselor so telling me his story was good for his image. My story seemed to sadden him. The disconnection from my parents was totally against the African way of life. He was affected. I wondered if I should tell people my story, most people have had hardships, I thought, just to varying degrees.

He told me that a life like mine makes one stronger, I agreed. I told him for the past two years, I committed to making myself happy hence I was in Brazil chilling. He said he respected me for coming to a foreign country alone, he said I had balls, I laughed! We cruised through Lapa with ease. It was most crowded, but unbeknownst to Sergio, I was used to it by now.

I took pics with the dread I bought 3 Orixa necklaces from, 2 last week and a new 1 tonight. I took pictures of the Lapa arches and the crowd, I bought a tee-shirt and earrings. Sergio took a picture of me and my sexy DANCE PARTNER Bobby Paz. Bobby was not happy to see Sergio (lol!) Sergio speaks English, Bobby does not and Sergio is there for me every day. Sergio bought me water and a lollipop, introduced me to all his Angolan friends. Showed me off a bit. I took pics with all of them, they were really cool and friendly too. One said he was a Bonga music producer and he told Sergio that he liked me and I could come to his house and burn all of his Bonga music if I wanted.

I put my arm around Sergio, pointed to him and said "me gusta Sergio!" The producer friend said he didn't like me like that but that I looked like a South African woman to him. Sergio told me the same thing on the bus ride there, that my complexion, height and build were reminiscent of a South African woman. Sergio told me that the guy made that statement about my looks without his input. The Bonga Producer took a picture of me standing with him with his digital camera but none of us could figure out how to retrieve the picture to look at it (lol!)

Day Eight

Sergio and I took the bus back and he walked me to my hotel about 4:30am, 5 kisses and 2 hugs later, we parted ways. I woke up determined to get to the Jardin Botanico, took Sergio's advice and had someone write me a note in Portuguese that said "I want to go to the Botanical Garden."

The note was written by a German tourist dude, he was so nice. I could tell that he was a little concerned for me because he insisted on walking me to the RIGHT bus stop. I just took his note and followed him to the bus stop. The note worked, it got me there, other people wanted to help, they were also telling me *which* bus to take when he left me at the bus stop. The money collector on the bus had me sit where he could tell me when to get off. It all worked perfectly.

I got to the garden, bus was 1.60 reals, the garden entrance fee was 4 reals. 5.60 reals is less than $2 in US dollars, the scenery was priceless. It was nearly all green exotic plants and the tallest trees ever, but only one flower patch- roses that you could smell when the wind blew. I had someone take a picture of me in the midst of them. I walked around and on the way out I bought postcards, a meditation CD and in the gift shop I was given a list of the bus numbers and told that I could catch any one of them back to my hotel, very easy. I took a public bus which put me off closer to my hotel than where I had originally caught the bus from.

I was happy, but I feel sick now, a sore throat has been nagging me for the past three days. I broke out in a full body, itchy, heat rash yesterday from over tanning which was still present today and as if things couldn't get any worse, an ear infection started coming on while I was still in the botanical garden. My ear got stuffy like I couldn't hear out of it, then it would hurt whenever I bent over or burped. The last time I had an ear infection was roughly two years ago when I juice fasted for 10 days, the pain of an ear infection is excruciating, the thought of which made me want to cry.

I fought back the tears fearing that the mucus build up would make my situation worse. Clumps of yellow/green mucus were coming out of my throat in the mornings when I woke and when I gagged while brushing my teeth. Yellow mucus came out when I blew my nose. Just a week ago in New York City I had a mild cold, but at least the mucus was clear then, now I feel tired, run down and unhappy.

Suddenly, it's too hot for me outside (somewhere between 90 -100 degrees but I can never tell because it's always shown in Celsius, not in Farenheit) and I was too far away from English speaking medics to be coming down with something so painful as an ear infection. I sat on a step while in the Botanical Garden and prayed. I knew I had been having raw salads and fruits daily, avocados, apples, coconut water and coconut jelly, beets, carrots and cabbage, but I was also indulging in bread, seafood, sweets, ice cream and pastries. I knew I had made myself sick. I'd had a sprout salad for lunch with squeezed lime and a pinch of salt as salad dressing and wondered when my full torso heat rash would go away. My arms and legs had cleared up already but my neck, tummy, and butt cheeks were still red and itchy with heat rash.

I was most upset because an ear infection generally requires a doctor's attention. I had no extra money and did not want to return back to New York before seeing Bahia. I knew I could heal myself if I tried. In the garden, spirit told me to eat raw garlic, water fast and visit the health food store for a lymph draining massage and nutritional supplements. I got to the health food store, Verde Mundo, and booked a 30 minute Shiatsu massage, bought Senna leaf and some other pills the clerk said was good for an ear infection. I bought 6 bottles of 1.5 liter water for roughly 50 cents each in US dollars. I taped positive words written on paper to the bottles of water as spirit had instructed me to do.

At night, I ate a clove of fresh garlic and stuffed my ear with another clove that I had bitten off the tip of. I would nap with a clove of garlic plugged in my ear. When I woke the first time, I removed it and noticed that the pain was gone and my ear was no longer clogged, until I burped, then the pain hit. I decided to take some of the ear infection herbs from the health food store, funny how they smelled like garlic. I took a double dose (4 capsules) and continued laying down. I only left the bed to use the bathroom and answer the phone. I wondered if Sergio would call or if he'd gotten the email I had sent him earlier. He finally called and we talked for a while. He said he thought about me, as if he were worried about me, but said he knew I was smart and would be okay. That's very interesting considering that he didn't know I was under the weather.

I told him I went to the garden all by myself on the bus and took pics and saw all the plants and how the garden looked like my dream especially when I saw a kid catching a fish with her hand and a net, how I bought a meditation CD and wanted to use his CD player and asked if we could see his music producer friend tomorrow and how I felt a cold coming on. He said he wanted to take me to Lapa again to take pictures of some famous, fancy stairs that one man, all alone, had decorated with beautiful tiles.

The stairs were like 3 flights high and the sides were all tiled as well. He said the music dude lived close to Lapa so we'd call him tomorrow and that he'd bring me his CD player, but I'd have to bring my own headphones. I told him that I got him something, he said to keep it as a surprise, it was from Verde Mundo, Aloe incense that was my favorite, I couldn't articulate what aloe was (in Portuguese or English) to Sergio, let's see if Sergio gets it when I give it to him. I asked pendulum if Sergio already had a girlfriend, pendulum said yes.

He told me to ask my pendulum if he should be my boyfriend. I told him I didn't need the pendulum to tell me that because as far as I was concerned he already was my boyfriend whether he liked me or not, we laughed. I told him that he was beautiful inside and out, was gracious, generous and had integrity and that I liked him because we could talk for days, hours and not run out of things to say. He didn't know what to say, he said thank you. I told him we could be friends it's not like we had sex just a little kissing.

We planned to meet the next day, he said 11am. I was shocked, that's really early I thought, he told me he sleeps until late afternoon. I accepted though I had just told him that I had laundry to do the next day. He said he would bring me medicine. I told him I bought herbs from Verde Mundo. He said if I didn't take his medicine he'd keep it because you never know when you'd get sick. We got off the phone agreeing to meet at 11am, but not having said where. I told him that was early for him. I felt flattered, maybe he'll call at 11 and we'll meet later on. In any event, I was happy that he wanted to see me earlier than usual. Am I giving myself enough credit?

I took the herbs before retiring for the night and had dreams that I think indicated the releasing of deep seated frustrations and annoyances. Even a past life was revealed to me, a situation of hostility based on racism that I was saved from. I was on a road trip with two white men. We stopped in the city to get me a warm coat which I used to cover myself in the back seat. We drove on a primitive, twisted road and had to eventually stop to put water in the carburetor. I got out and looked around. Old, western, white men on foot and horses were slowly making their way through the dirt road/desert, some looked at me and sneered at the white men I was with as if to say, "if you weren't here I'd hurt her." I felt the fear and one f my roadies told me to hurry up and get back in the car. Even he seemed scared and hopped in. I think this and other dreams represented angers and fears I had been holding on to and since I had the shiatsu and Senna leaf, those repressed, negative emotions were released through the dreams like a cloud of smoke.

Day Nine

I was weak when I awoke, but managed to get myself together. I decided to give Sergio thirty minutes to call me before I ventured out and called him later. At 11:15am it looked like rain, damn, that would push our plans back, no bother though I could do laundry and develop pictures, buy more film and have a salad. I bought an umbrella and everything I needed was local anyway. Sergio and I did meet today. I did laundry using my credit card but did not develop any rolls of film. Need to wait until a money wire comes in. I had watermelon for breakfast and avocado for lunch. I met a nice English speaking Portuguese woman named Denise at the Laundromat. We talked about Bahia, she gave me her phone number and told me to call her should I need anything while still in Rio and I gave her my number and told her to do the same. I stayed pretty close to the hotel and still wasn't feeling well. Denise had given me the bus numbers and instructions to Rio Sul- a mall where I could have developed film today because it was a Sunday and everything else around us was closed. I wrote down her instructions knowing that I would not go today and knowing that Sergio had already shown me the way. I wanted to go alone though.

Sergio and I met up around 3pm, after playing phone tag, he overslept through his alarm. Sergio took me to Lapa so I could see Selaron's public works of art that spanned an entire enclave. It ended in a massive re-edification of stairs (over 200 of them.) Some of the tiles were hand painted in detail, some were intentionally broken into pieces by the artist for aesthetic purposes, I presume. It was all so awesome, Sergio took pictures of me sitting on the staircase and I took close ups of the tiles to appreciate later. Sergio had promised we'd see his music producer friend to burn me some Bonga music. We got on a bus out of Lapa and I reminded him. He looked upset and said that he had honestly forgotten. He took me to Rio Sul instead, how intuitive, I thought, of him to take me where I'd planned to go anyway, he's in tune like that, very wise.

In the mall I shopped, eventually buying a shirt, scarf and mesh pocketbook. I pledged to return for a large leather pocketbook that I saw on sale for like $63US. Sergio walked me back to my hotel courtyard where we politicked for hours, literally until 1:30am. A guy named Daniel who was staying at my hotel got into our debate over the plight of Black people. Daniel was Ethiopian and answered questions I had incorrectly answered to Sergio earlier. Sergio and I argued passionately "that's bullshit!" Until Daniel left, then we spoke affectionately again. He had told Daniel that he would marry me and we would have kids. I was speechless and joked that he was my first baby since he wanted four kids and I wanted three. We parted at 1:45am like two kids who didn't want to stop playing but whose eyelids were getting heavy. Sergio promised to take me to the music dude the next day.

Day Ten

Sergio called me early this time. He had business to take care of and said he wouldn't be late today. We met pretty early for him, roughly 11am and headed downtown. I don't know what he went to do, but I tried retrieving money through Western Union with just my passport and was told that I needed a control number. We went to a flea market like shopping area where I bought nothing because Sergio bought things for me. He bought me like 10 necklaces and 4 blank CD's to burn on for later. We met his friend and ex-roommate Armando, a nice looking tall brother from Angola, and married father of two. He was very pleasant. We three went to the music dude's house and they tried to burn me some music for like two hours. The program was not responding to Sergio's blank CD's. I took pictures of these beautiful, gracious, generous, patient people and we left. Sergio promised we'd return tomorrow to pick up the CD's once they figured out the problem.

The three of us left to eat at a restaurant. The food: vegetable rice, mashed potatoes and fried salmon in tomato and shrimp sauce was slamming. I ordered a salad which turned out to be rife with pork, turkey, mayonnaise and some other things I did not want to eat. I picked so much shit out of it that Sergio finally said "Don't eat it." He said they may charge us for the salad but no bother. I was glad. I didn't want to look bad for wasting food.

The waiter served us from huge platters that appeared to grand for one person. Armando or Sergio must have specified that the order was for three people, I wonder. The food was awesome, delicious. We must have sat there for 3 or 4 hours politicking, rapping and just chilling. The police rolled up with huge, massive, dirty rifles out in hand when they came into the restaurant to eat. I asked Sergio if I may take a picture of them, he said "no" with a firm look in his eye, rather fatherly I thought.

About half an hour later I got up to take a picture of Sergio, Armando and a rapper friend of theirs arguing about the purity of modern hip hop. Sergio stopped and looked at me, getting up from my seat fidgeting with my camera. "What are you doing?" He demanded to know as if I were a child running towards the street. "Taking a picture of you" I said sweetly. I was busted. I wanted to sneak a snap shot of the police, he returned to his conversation with the rapper dude in broken Portuguese, their native Angolan tongue and slang.

He was so sexy in his style of dress, depth of voice and passion for his people and his beliefs. For a long time, Sergio talked with his friends in foreign dialects, often apologizing and filling me in on conversation points, once he asked me my opinion in an objective context. I chose a point of view that obviously wasn't his because he went back to the debate as if I hadn't said a word, still sexy in his masculinity. All the way back on the bus he drilled me on his point. I still had a differing point of view. Armando felt sorry for me, looking into my eyes he said softly in English "Are you sleepy?" I said "yes."

Sergio kind of took the hint. We three walked to my hotel where Sergio and I exchanged the Brazilian kiss-kiss, we had been improvising on it to three kisses total and at least two hugs. Sergio had figured out that I wasn't really taller than him, it just seemed that way until we were back to back or shoulder to shoulder, then he had ¾ to an inch on me. It made him stronger. He and Armando left me roughly between 10 and 11pm. *Good*, I thought, *this way we'll each get a decent night's sleep.*

Sergio said he'd call me in the morning. I told him to make it noon, this way if he overslept or was late, I'd have things done for myself and not feel dependent on something that may not happen, like him forgetting to put my film in today as promised. We had spent the entire day in inconvenient locations so I wasn't mad at him, the opportunity had not presented itself and I knew it was expensive to develop eight rolls of film anyway. I didn't want him to be responsible. I reminded him when it was too late that I wanted to put the film in so I could show him the pictures before I left Rio for Bahia. I was supposed to be back in NYC like 2 days ago. Whatever, we parted roughly midnight promising to call each other around noon.

Day Eleven

I got up around 8am, showered, dressed and headed out to check emails, drop off film, pick up a money transfer and buy the leather pocketbook from Rio Sul. I did all of those things except for pick up the money because the line was too long first thing in the morning. I had Sergio meet me at the bank, knowing there'd be a wait. He entered when I got in front of the teller. She refused me the transaction after all because the sender had spelled my name wrong by one letter (Hinson), Sergio and I were outraged. Sergio argued with the woman and we left. He said we'd find another location. We met with Armando to go downtown and to an island off of Rio where the rich people lived because it was beach front and there was no crime. First we went to another bank where I received the wire transfer and then we caught the ferry to the Museum of Contemporary Art, which looks like a spaceship that was built on top of the ocean water with an amazing view from the inside. The island is called Niteroi.

We could see people fishing right below us through the window as if it were the most natural thing in the world. Sergio said it was best to live like this. We joked on the exhibits then went walking along the beach until it started to rain. We took an autobus back after Armando asked me if I wanted another ferry ride or bus ride back, I said bus. I had taken enough pictures of and on the ferry and I wanted to sit the hell down now! I knew they were exposing me to the most beautiful sights around and did not complain.

Sergio teased me saying that I was walking so fast and he asked me if I was walking back to NY. We laughed and I told him that I thought I was walking slow! Sergio and I both fell asleep on the ride back, it was so long! My left shoulder was killing me, I looked unhappy trying to sit up straight in seats that were not spaced enough for my long legs. I told Sergio my shoulder hurt, he massaged it. I told him I didn't want to leave but had to, he said he regretted not having his own place for me to stay with him. I asked him how long it would take him to get to NY, he said 6 months to get organized, renew his passport and tie up loose strings. I rudely showed my dismay, "6 months?" He said "you'll forget me," "no," I said, "never." And I meant it. I knew my heart would long for him and for Rio- equally. He said I should come back to Rio between then. I told him the trip cost me over $2,000.

He was surprised probably that I'd spent that much on a vacation. I told him I was in Brazil following my dreams. I told him about the dreams I had two nights in a row days ago. He knew I wasn't crazy. He said he respected me for being there alone. I was eternally grateful for his companionship, guidance, wisdom and protection.

Armando asked me not to forget him. I told him, "how could I, you've fed me."

Armando had been paying for Sergio and I to eat, take transportation and access the museum. They wouldn't LET me pay for anything. It wasn't even weird that Armando was paying. They were like one, Armando being an extension of Sergio, not two individuals. It was beautiful and they were beautiful, complementing each other like words with music. Sergio was the words, he was aggressive and outgoing, Armando was the music, flowing gently and calmly. We were poetry in motion. They collectively and individually treated me like a queen. One held my bags, Sergio had been for the past few days, while the other held my food/beverage. They would switch depending on the situation. No question, I walked slightly ahead of them or nestled in between them absorbing their dialects. Not listening with my ears but, able to laugh when they did as if riding the vibration, the emotion, not the verbal expression, energy traveled through us like waves, we even yawned together, we three were compatible.

I was impressed and flattered by their attentiveness and invited them both to come to NYC anytime, together. Sergio had taken the most beautiful picture I had ever seen of myself in the restaurant the day before it was (strangely, I thought) his perception of me. I told him that I didn't know I was so beautiful. They started walking me to my hotel, but I stopped them and said I was going to Verde Mundo for a massage. Armando agreed saying "yes, rest, you're flying out to Bahia tomorrow."

Sergio joked that his massage on the bus ride wasn't good enough, he clapped his hands and said he would give me a real deal massage when he got to NYC. We had agreed on several occasions that we saw each other fit for a real relationship. I wondered often what it would take to transcend, we were in tune like nobody's business. I can't deny the chemistry, the ease, the innocence, the mystique surrounding us. Ray, my buddy from Brooklyn, had said before I left, that I would meet my husband in Rio, damn he's good. Sergio and Armando left me at Mundo Verde at about 6pm. I got a massage and picked up the pictures, matches for my incense and drinking water on the way back to the hotel. I took a picture of the massage dude, Wilson, he was fine as hell and he gave me his email address after I tipped him $5R reals = $2US. I was exhausted and them brothers could walk! They knew I was tired.

Sergio promised to call me, but by 11:41pm he still hadn't. I asked him out on a date tonight for dinner and a movie, he blushed. I thought he accepted, apparently, he hadn't. Earlier I had offered to buy him a book, he declined profusely. I told him we should meet early the next morning since I was flying out fo' shizzle. I'd asked him to come with me and he said he wished he could. There was a moment of sadness between us. I think I am in love again, if not he is the prototype.

Day Twelve

I looked at and organized the now developed pictures into given books- foto albums. Looking at the pictures had me bawling like a baby because I did not want to leave Rio or Sergio and never leave Brazil for that matter! I fell asleep listening to R&B music. Woke at 6:30am, got up at 7:30, showered at 8, left the hotel at 9, bought a duffel bag and lotsa gifts for designating when I return to NY. Perhaps I spent way too much! Anyhow, after retrieving a Western Union transfer and booking a round trip flight from Rio to Bahia and back to Rio for like $100 USD, I learned it would cost me a solid grand in USD to get back to NYC since I had overstayed and missed my original flight back. There was no way around it! To get home I would need a "Free Ayana" money campaign.

Parting Rio for Bahia was such sweet sorrow. Sergio and I caught up roughly 3:30pm. I was tense and uptight, disappointed that it would cost me so much to get home. Sergio was cool as a cucumber and he talked me through it ultimately telling me it was my fault for not paying attention to the details. He was right, I was shocked. All the books I read, all the courses I paid for to take and here he was telling me I was at the source of it all in a way I could accept like good coaching.

He went with me to the travel agency to figure out a cheaper way- to no avail. He offered to cover me for two nights in Rio if I needed to in order to get back to NY and couldn't straight from Salvador, Bahia. There are no flights from Salvador to NY we found out. I was relieved that someone had my back out here in the world, it was comforting. I told Sergio I was hungry and would be able to relax once I ate some food. I told him that I wanted to take him out to dinner.

Sergio and I found a nice buffet restaurant to eat at. I piled my plate high while he delicately arranged his food (sushi) on a plate. He saw my plate and asked if it was all I could eat or if I would come back for seconds. I became embarrassed at the pile of assorted foods on my plate in comparison to his neatly arranged one and said "oh, wow, you have a point, I should come back for seconds, instead of piling my plate high now!" We laughed at me but it wasn't his point or he had another, he said it may be cheaper to weigh my plate than to pay the flat rate, "no" I said, "I agreed to pay the buffet rate and I will come back for more food too."

We ate and had fascinating conversations causing each other to laugh out loud several times.

We even talked about past lives. I asked him if he'd been a woman in a past life, because he was adamant about women having children under any circumstances. He said that he paid 50 cent for a past life reading and got a message that he'd been a Russian woman in a past life. I laughed 'til I cried. We made each other laugh with the slightest gesture knowing that something funny was about to be said or happen. He looked at all the pictures I took and praised my photography skills. I gave him a small yoga book, because he'd said days earlier that he wanted to learn yoga, and a card that read in Portuguese "you have completely conquered...my heart. I wrote in Portuguese inside the card "My love, it was my pleasure to meet you, you are a good, kind, pretty/handsome (bonita,) interesting conversationalist, mind sex! And my heart is yours until next time."

I wrote my name, address, phone numbers and email addresses for him and I put the full meaning of my name. I wrote in English "Don't forget me, I will wait for you in NY." I am in love with Sergio, we got along too well to be true. He walked me to the hotel and we sat and talked for a long time. I took a deep breath and he said "what, what are you going to say?" I looked down, too shy to say anything. I played it off like "nothing" but he was on to me. "What?" I told him "okay," I took another deep breath, "I appreciate you and your friends looking out for me, your kindness, generosity and graciousness." I told him how he made my trip transformative and that I had planned to spend most of my time at the beach and he showed me everything that wasn't on the map and that his friends were most gracious and generous especially Armando and how we three were so in tune that we yawned together and that I laughed on key with them while walking between though they spoke in broken Portuguese and Angolan dialects and slang.

I told him that Armando was like his arm or leg, an extension of him and how Armando was there but not there and how Armando and I could talk easily and how he and Armando were like interchangeable persons, like ghosts or shadows of each other. It was amazing to see them in action. Sergio appeared jealous that I spoke of Armando at length, I switched back to him. Come to NY soon. I told him that I would take care of him. He said he wanted to say a lot of things to me but he said "my English is not helping me," we laughed. I told him it was okay. Clearly he had shown me enough to know that he was sincere. I felt for him because it looked like he wanted to say a lot but couldn't for whatever reasons.

Finally he said, "I want you, I did not hug or kiss you because I did not want to be your vacation. I like how our relation(ship) is going, I wanted to kiss you or hug you many times, it is better to get to know each other before you kiss and hug and no longer like the person after." I told him about the

"Science of Love" and how people "fall in love" with the projection of their ideal on to another which is why people quickly fall out of love, as I spoke Sergio said "exactly, exactly."

I asked him what he saw possible. He said a serious relationship, a commitment that he would take very seriously. I agreed, "a long term relationship," I said and I told him he would make me a life partner because that's what I saw him as. He was quiet. I asked him if I was too forward, he said no it was good for a woman to express her feelings for a man and that not enough do. He said our meeting and subsequent encounters were like we'd met before in another time and place, like old friends who had met again. I was stunned. He had earlier, at the buffet restaurant, said that I was very open minded and that for him to talk with someone very intelligent had caused him to know things and say things he had never heard or thought he knew before.

I told him he was in tune and a righteous man because he was tapping into collective consciousness. And thoughts were waves of energy that we catch onto when righteous and in tune. I told him we could know everything in the whole, wide world and universe if we tapped into this collective consciousness. He said he believed in the power of the mind, that if one thought he could fly, he would. I was impressed. Sergio is profoundly intuitive, he catches my thoughts out of thin air.

Later I told him that he was saying things I had held back and bringing up conversations I was about to initiate and completing thoughts I had left open from the day before, he looked happy. Sergio was happy. I'd given him the yoga book and refused to open the card in my presence, he said that he'd save the best for last and even read my emails last. He said he'd read the card at night before he went to bed. I told him I liked to rip shit open immediately, he laughed. I told him I'd try not to pressure him or offer to open it for him, we laughed. I started to cry when I was telling him that I was glad to have met him and he said this was why he did not like parting. We hugged and kissed face, neck, finally lips before I got in the cab, he told me to email him daily from Bahia, I promised to.

Day Thirteen

I landed in Bahia at 2am, took a cab to a hotel that I found in a phone book at the baggage claim, fell asleep in the cab until I got there. Checked in at Pelourinho Hotel and crashed for the night. I strongly sensed that there was both a female and a male ghost in the hotel room with me observing me. I tuned them out and let my iPod put me to sleep.

I got up around noon and spent the next two hours sending out "I'm safe" emails and details on my whereabouts. I finally went outside and found that my hotel was on a strip of restaurants, art houses, boutiques and museums. All the buildings were colorful and historic in architecture. Things I had wanted to buy in Rio were cheaper in Bahia. Capoeira pants, Brazil T shirts, and crystal bangles were in abundance. I was totally wide eyed and amazed. I walked around in short- shorts and I felt uncomfortable as if I stood out among the people. People were generally fully dressed.

Men were lusting after me in a pretty primitive way. I felt very uncomfortable. I considered asking someone if was appropriately dressed, then I decided against it. I took pictures of the streets, the people, the buildings, the art work. I asked around where I could learn Capoeira. I was directed to a school, where I went and asked. He gave me a flyer and said there was a demo at 8pm. In twenty minutes. I ran back to my hotel to drop stuff off, then I went back to the dojo. No luck, $15R's to get in. I had nothing, he turned me away. I watched people playing Capoeira in the street, a teacher emerged and pulled me into the circle to play with him, I did. Then I arranged to meet with an instructor from their crew the next day for $20R for 2 hours. His name was Pantera Negra and he was very tall and dark skinned. I was very happy.

Day Fourteen

At 10am met Pantera Negra my new capoeira instructor and we went to spar in the space under a tilted cross. Under this cross we played capoeira. I was instructed to properly stretch for quite some time, then we started to play. The instructor gave frequent 30 second to 1 minute breaks. I was grateful for them but dared not request them. He only spoke Portuguese so it was hard for me to understand him. I had to watch and learn. A lot of moves were similar to Wu Shu Kwan and Ife martial arts I took a couple of years back, I was glad for that.

We dripped sweat the whole time, then there was stretching after the capoeira lesson was done where he'd try to break my arms and legs by stretching them out until I screamed, whined or beat his chest. He took me back to where we met and he looked for an interpreter to help us to talk. He found a man named Joshua who was a museum tour guide. Joshua, a native Brazilian who spoke fluent English, told me to come back and meet Pantera at the same place at 3pm. He wanted to take me to the beach, I agreed. Pantera left, Joshua insisted that I speak with him and his English student Katya, a young, shy girl who appeared tired of studying English. We talked a bit, I asked her to exchange my English lessons for her Portuguese lessons while we walked the museums.

We three happily agreed to this. Joshua offered his home, a three bedroom apartment to me, I joyfully accepted. I could save lots of money this way. Joshua also offered to take me to Candomble, an African spiritual tradition done in praise of the Orishas, for $35 Reals. I agreed. I told him I would shower, redress and return. Then the girl could show me the museums while we conversed in English and Portuguese. We had a deal, I ran off to change because I was sweaty as hell. By the time I returned the entire center was closed and would not reopen until 2pm. Since I was meeting Pantera Negra at 3pm, I visited the museums. You can see all 10 of them in 3 hours. I took pictures where I could and went back to meet Pantera at 3pm. He was not there so I did not wait. Many guys were sitting around and I did not feel comfortable waiting around so I left.

I walked the streets taking pictures, visiting art houses and galleries. I came across the garment district where all the fabrics seemed like they were for upholstery. I grew tired and found a restaurant to eat at near my hotel. This was the third restaurant I had eaten at in Bahia. It was formal and pricey at $20 per plate, which is like $60 to a Brazilian. The food was piled high and it was worth it, excellent grilled salmon, black eyed peas and white rice with chopped broccoli in it. The day before I ate for nearly half that price and the food was great and lunch for even half the latter was excellent at a place where you pay for food by weight. There I had fish, rice, beans and salad for the US dollar equivalent of $2.50 at most. Mmm! Mmm! Was surprised that price did not affect quality! Anyhow, I had more than a couple of caipirinhas with my meal and I collapsed once I got in.

Day Fifteen

Met Pantera again for capoeira at 10am. He was late so Joshua bade me enter his museum and wait. I explained to him that I took too long to come back and everything was closed. He said he'd waited outside, I apologized profusely. The truth is I had gotten held up due to arguing with the hotel staff over an iron that I refused to pay for using and it made me late. Pantera showed up 20 minutes late. Joshua requested that I return at noon to learn Portuguese. I was grateful for Joshua as he was one of few people in Bahia who spoke fluent English. Pantera and I waited in the museum until it stopped raining outside, then we went back under the cross where we played the day before. It rained off and on, I dared not ask for a break since we were dripping sweat anyway.

Amazingly, the cross significantly protected us from the rainfall. I enjoyed playing like that. Joshua had asked me to return so after Pantera showed me the elevator that cost about 5 cents in Brazilian money to ride, a huge marketplace and center where his school played capoeira for contributions, I told him to return me to Joshua. I was late again. Joshua sat with me and discussed personal pronouns and taught me how to say my name and where I am from. He wrote it down for me. I promised to send him English books so that he may practice and teach. He reminded me of our appointment to go to Candomble tonight. I was to meet him at 6:40pm in my hotel lobby.

I was late from checking my emails to meet him. Joshua came back for me and off we went to pick up others from hotels and hostels for the Candomble. It was a lengthy ceremony. I didn't feel or notice anything different except for the brightness of the stars afterward. Joshua took me to his home so I could consider staying with him. After Candomble, I went to his 3 bedroom apartment. Long story short, the bathroom didn't suit me. There was a toilet bowl, but no seat cover. There was no separation between the shower and the toilet. There was just a big room that was the whole bathroom. I agreed to spend the night, it was midnight or later and there were no street lights outside, but when I went to shower, I realized that my menses had come down. Damn, could it have been a result of the Candomble ceremony?

I was thinking of my dear friend Sehu (the Brooklyn monk) words during the ceremony from when he said women don't have to make animal sacrifices, our monthly cycle is good enough to count as a sacrifice. Low and behold, I thought it, so it was.

I told Joshua that I had to go to my hotel for my feminine hygiene products. He gave me $10 for a cab, walked me to the cab corner and waved down a taxi for me. I was relieved to get to the hotel and plotted a story to give Joshua as to why I could not stay with him.

Day Sixteen

I saw Joshua this morning while going to meet Pantera Negra for Capoeira. Pantera was running late and Joshua wanted to talk. I told him I could not stay with him because he lived too far from the main square and I would want to come in late from parties. He said it was no problem but for me it was cab fare and a hassle because he had no bell. Ultimately he accepted my refusal although he was offended. He said he wanted to exchange my stay at his place and he would stay with me in NYC! Huh!

I trained in capoeira every day more intense than the day before, sometimes I thought Pantera was mad at me because he'd train really hard and be rough about some things. One session he refused to give me breaks. Another time he eased up and invited me to his house and we tried our damnedest to communicate, it was funny. He offered me to stay with him, but I declined after observing the conditions. But I left the Pelourhino Hotel after Pantera told me I was paying too much.

Pastel, the capoeira pack leader and Pantera Negra's friend, told him to bring me to his hotel "Chile" for $20 Reals per night with breakfast included. I agreed and moved to that hotel. I was happy to be saving $50 Reals per night, until their doorman got too friendly with me and groped me late one night as I stumbled in tipsy from a club. Then I went to stay with an older woman for 24 Reals per night. I was referred to her by an information guide. Her neighborhood was shady, it looked like Brooklyn in the 1800's. I visited all the museums in Pelourhino, they say you can do all of Pelourhino in two days, and it's true.

I met some young people, some of whom spoke English, most of whom did not. All of the cute guys don't speak English, at least the 3 very fine men I desperately tried to talk to without getting anywhere, how frustrating. The young people who speak English here are very politically astute and aware of the problems where they are. They know about and love the rappers "dead prez." They know about racism in America. They respect Black American culture and work hard to preserve the styles, dance and arts, they apologized to me for the anti-female tone to modern hip hop and wanted to know if hip hop really is dead (as if I know the answer.) These young men that I just met, took me to a "Women's Day" feminist-like rally. I didn't even realize what it was until we got there and the place was packed with women. All the speakers talked in Portuguese but the only men I saw were the ones who brought me. I took pictures.

The young people who speak English teach the rest. I promised a young Bahian male that I would send him an English dictionary and some books. I received money to return to NY from friends and my brother was depositing the checks into my account. I decided to return to Rio de Janeiro as that was the best way out of Brazil and I wanted to see Sergio again before returning to the US. He and I had been in communication by phone a few times while I was in Bahia.

I would call Sergio and give him the number where I was staying and we would pick a time of day to talk that I would be by the phone waiting on his call. And it worked, we talked about my experiences in Bahia and he sounded pretty worried about me which made me want to see him again even more. I cried on the cab ride out of Bahia on the way back to the airport. There was so much beauty in that place, and a richness of spirit about the people. I noticed a circular cluster of iron statues of Orisha goddesses in action poses, like they were people walking on water, in the center of the lake. It was then that I realized that the Orishas were all female goddesses in Bahia unlike in the replication of this religion in America known as Yoruba where some of the deities are male and the culture is male dominant to the point of the exclusion of women from high priest positions. In Bahia, the Orishas are represented in every form of artistic expression, always in the feminine aspect and dress.

I prayed on it and decided to step out on faith by spending all of my pocket money while in Bahia on 5 paintings, clothes, jewelry like crystal rings and bracelets. I bought so much stuff that I had to mail some of it back to my Brooklyn address in the US from Bahia- a difficult venture.

Day Seventeen

Joshua saw me at a museum, he is a tour guide taking tourists to different museums, he said that the young lady he introduced me to, Katya, wanted me to go to her house and meet her family for dinner. Katya thought I was avoiding her. I wasn't keeping up with our English – Portuguese barter. I went to the museum where Katya studied English, she told me to go home with her on the spot. I was sweaty, dirty, sandy from playing capoeira on the beach with Pantera Negra but she insisted that I go home with her, in her limited English. I told her a few days ago that I was vegetarian, this is why I sorta avoided accepting her dinner invitations. She wouldn't take no for an answer. We rode the bus for about an hour away from the Pelourinho tourist area. It was all dirt roads and chickens were running around freely. We got to her house, very clean, the whole family was there with so many people. "HI!" they shouted in unison, talked my head off in Portuguese I smiled, laughed and nodded.

Katya gave me a change of clothes, soap, towel and washcloth and led me to the bathroom where I took a shower, the family was at the dinner table. They were happy to see me, "HI!" everybody said again. We ate from mountainous food platters. Katya's mom had a vegetarian cook book on the kitchen counter, she had made me 3 different vegetarian dishes and several salads. Mom served me first, carefully placing only the vegetarian items on my plate. Then she cut up all the meats and served those out to everyone, everyone else had to serve their own sides, except me. Mom knew which sides had meat in them and which sides did not.

After dinner mom took me to her bedroom and asked me, in Portuguese, to take a nap, I obliged waking up two hours later totally disoriented, it was pitch black. I left mom's bedroom and went back to the living room, the family was watching Portuguese soap operas. Again in unison they said "HI!" like it was the first time we were meeting, it was funny and charming, they were excited to see me. Mom tried to feed me dessert. I asked Katya to take me to the bus stop. I had a wonderful time and will miss them a lot.

I was scared for myself and for Katya too, we were walking in the complete dark outside, looking for the bus stop, it was something I did not want to do but I felt like getting back into the tourist area. Katya bought me some food along the walk, it was a large piece of corn bread stuffed with okra and shrimp stew. I was overwhelmed by her generosity, I had just eaten myself into a coma at her house and here she was sending me off with more food. The bus came quickly. I boarded it and made it back to the area I was familiar with without a problem.

Day Eighteen

Pantera Negras is mad at me for being late again this morning. After a rough work out I feel like the karate kid. Pantera found a stick about as tall as me and drove it into the beach sand, then made me kick over it at least a hundred times with each leg. All he says is "Agora! Agora! Agora!" I instinctively knew what it meant, it's like saying "do it again, again" again and again, keep kicking every time he says Agora! I had learned early on that with Pantera smiling, laughing, whining, whimpering or crying would get me prolonged training, extra time running up and down the beach and limb tearing stretches. He had no sympathy and looked at my signs of weakness with disgust. Face to face, I would speed up the rhythm of my movements, instead of following his lead and "accidentally" kick the shit out of him when while we play capoeira, technically a no-contact spar, he didn't seem to notice.

After practice Pantera and I met up with his capoeira crew and and we'd all go to the beach or a restaurant and just hang out. Pantera was very quiet and shy, he'd stay by my side and always sit next to me on the bus or whatever but he did not really try to speak to me. When we were not playing capoeira, Pantera was a calm and gentle soul with innocent eyes. The other guys in his crew constantly bust his balls and he's like really passive.

Physically he was the tallest, biggest and darkest but he wasn't aggressive at all.

Day Nineteen

Finally! Broke the communication barrier between me and Pantera, told him I wanted to go see the large turtles I had dreamt about, the tartarugas, he didn't know what the hell I was talking about at first but I had some Brazilian money that had the turtles pictured on them. Immediately, we headed to the place where the turtles were bred and released to the ocean to keep them from going extinct. It was a 2 hour ride away from the tourist area. It was an outdoor place with swimming pools with different sized turtles and it was designed to educate the tourists on the turtles' endangered plight. Spent a few hours there, did a little shopping and headed back to Pelourinho.

Pantera is so nice when we are not sparring he just rolls around with me like he doesn't have a care in the world. This is the magic of Brazilians, they seem to be on vacation too. Brazilians do stop and talk to me in the street and don't give up until we reach some kind of understanding, they are very patient; always trying to take me home with them but not in a perverted or criminal way. They just want me to have a good time and will come out of their pockets to see to it that I do.

Day Twenty

Capoeira in the morning then a boring day spent at internet cafes and gelato shops, tonight I showered, dressed and headed out to the club alone. Met some young people in the club, no English as usual but the vibe was good. They kept buying rounds of beer. I got drunk. Out of nowhere, Pastel, the leader of the capoeira crew I play with during the day comes out of the club behind me, after a brief chat he gets in the cab with me and escorts me all the way home. I was so drunk he had to take my keys and unlock the doors for me. There's like three doors and each had at least two locks on them to get in. Actually there's a gate, a main entrance and my apartment door each with two locks because it was the 'hood. As we were fumbling with the keys, someone threw a rock that broke a street light bulb down the block. Pastel may well have saved my life.

Day Twenty One

Hung over, won't go to the square to meet Pantera today. Feeling so bad, I know he's waiting for me to show up. He'll wait for a long time before he gives up. Such a man. Wish I had a way to communicate to him, not gonna make it. Sorry Pantera, sorry to disappoint you.

The woman who is renting me a bed room in her apartment is taking care of me. She prepares me fresh fruit every morning, with bread and tea or coffee. She talks to me but I don't understand. I suspect that she wants to know how my trip is going. We talk for about 30 minutes or more everyday at the kitchen table either in the morning or evening, I have no idea what we are talking about. It's the thought that counts.

I have made some mistakes, like flooding her bathroom floor as I mindlessly showered without removing the plug from the drain first. She was very forgiving. I'm sure I've done other stupid things but she can't tell me what they are or maybe that's what she is trying to say to me every day. All I know is she is always happy to see me and wants to keep talking. She is only charging me a few dollars per day to stay with her and doesn't want me to leave.

I don't think she minded that Pastel brought me home last night. She didn't mention it.

Day Twenty Two

After morning capoeira, Pantera took me to the post office. I mailed back to my Brooklyn apartment two big boxes of stuff that I bought in Bahia. It'll take a few weeks to deliver and I'll be home in NYC way before then.

Pantera knows I am leaving Bahia tomorrow, he gave me a tee shirt so I can show that I am a student from his crew. I feel so proud of myself for earning this tee shirt, I will never wear it so as not to dirty it but I will show it off as a badge of honor.

Said my goodbyes to Pantera Negra, Pastel and another capoeira mestre name Yoji, they have all shown me a good time in Bahia from seriousness to play time. They kept me safe. Bahia is a spiritual vortex. I am complete here all day, every day. My heart is open here. I am cradled in the arms of God here. Crying enroute to the airport. Don't want to leave Bahia.

Day Twenty Three

I returned to Rio, to the same hotel with an upgraded room because I went from having nothing to having $2,000 in US dollars in my possession. I met up with Sergio but I was a different person now only ten days later. For starters I was much more grounded, happier, calmer and much more tanned. I was toned, slimmer and more muscular too. My Brazilian accent was beginning to kick in and my spirit had been humbled by the poverty I was exposed to from visiting people's homes in Bahia. Sergio was much more into me this time around he was clearly more attracted to me. I was ten times more confident and I had money to spare. Sergio accompanied me to pick up this large sum of money. I gave him $300 Reals, roughly $100 US dollars, especially due to all the money he and his friend Armando spent on me two weeks before, he seemed embarrassed and pretty much turned the money down. I insisted he take it and he said he would hold it for me and that I should leave all of my money at my hotel and he would spend the $300 Reals I had just given him, on me. What a man I thought, he's going to take the money I gave him and spend it on me. Good idea. And we had fun, I was free as a bird, even invited him into my hotel room. He laid on his back on the bed and we made conversation, but nothing sexual happened.

Day Twenty Four

Sergio finally got his chance to take me to see the movie *Million Dollar Baby*. It was in English with Portuguese sub-titles thank God. We went to dinner, walked on the beach. Finally, I am familiar with basic Portuguese language and can make casual conversation. Drawing in the sand and making hand gestures were my best attempts most days. I also can tell where I am going in Rio and how to get back to where I came from without asking for help.

Sergio and I have established places where we meet, we don't need to specify addresses or times of day. Now it seems like I have known Sergio for years. He is no longer my guide, I am a local Brazilian at this point. Once I tell people that I have been in the country for more than three weeks now, they don't try to speak my weird Spanglish anymore they just try to force me to speak in fluent Portuguese. I get it, it's like a joke indicating that I should know how to speak Portuguese by now. Even the other tourists aren't buying my wimpy "help me" bit anymore.

Day Twenty Five

Sad day, bought my return ticket back to NYC. Perhaps I should stay here and become an English teacher. I love this place, the people, the food, the music and the culture. Certainly Brazilians are more civilized than the people in NYC. Everyone's so easy to get along with.

Everywhere I go I see people loving on each other in public. I saw a young male teenager, holding hands with an old woman, like a grandmother. At first I thought, *Is that his girlfriend?* But then I realized that he was just a teenager walking with his grandma. There is no shame in that here. Also, in the banks and in the markets where there are long lines, senior citizens walk right up to the front of the lines. It's very natural, no one objects.

I've seen men hugging and kissing their children pretty much every where I've been in Brazil. I haven't seen that many men out in public, enjoying quality time with their children in NYC. I have never seen such bold acts of affection from men towards their family members as I have seen as a common occurrence in Brazil.

I thought it was mandatory that I came to Rio "bikini ready" before stretching out on the beach but on the beach I see a lot of older and overweight people CHILLING in their bikinis and Speedos. There is no judgment here. Brazilian people are sexy but not perverted. Brazilian people really want to get to know you. No one here has asked me for anything, except for the beggars in the tourist areas. Overall, Brazilian's are relaxed. If you are poor, fat, or have crooked teeth no one's going to judge any of that like they would in NYC.

Day Twenty Six

I'm not so mad at Jamal anymore for what he may or may not have done with a prostitute like 3 weeks ago. Forgot that he even existed, though he is the one who invited me here. Sent him an email saying "Haha! I'm still in Rio, went to Bahia and came back to Rio. Took lotsa pics. Be back in NYC soon." I attached a few pics so he'd know I wasn't lying.

It's a good thing we fell out a few weeks ago, it enabled me to go places and do things that he forbade me to do, like going out alone at night, visiting the favelas, going to people's houses and venturing outside of the tourist areas. I knew he'd be shocked to learn that I had the cahunas to fly over to Bahia days after his return to NYC.

I've learned something about sex tourism. I am not as offended by it as much as I initially was. Brazilian people in general are so sweet that I can totally understand how an American man would want to marry a Brazilian woman even if he met her under shady circumstances. The Brazilian lady is very relaxed and celebratory of life. Generosity of spirit is the status quo. People here are very compassionate, gentle and soft spoken.

Bahia is more country like compared to Rio which is definitely a city. Rio satisfies all of your physical senses. Bahia satisfied my soul. Bahia was like a spiritual vortex. In Bahia, I felt the Great Presence. I felt whole and complete. There was less stimulation, way less English speaking people but all of the contentment I have ever felt while doing nothing.

I'm not journaling for the next and last 2 days of my trip. Going to stay present to Rio, Brazil and Sergio. My heart is growing heavier as the time to leave grows nearer. Can't write anymore just want to live in the moment. Time is now precious.

Finally, I understand where I am, how to get around, communicate with others and live on very little resources and it's time to leave.

Chapter 7: All That Glitters

Being back in NYC was nothing short of culture shock. For starters it was really cold in NYC as compared to the summery weather I had enjoyed for a month in Brazil. I had a deep tan and noticed the paleness of my friends at my "Welcome Home" party. On the public bus and train people in NYC seemed to be dead on the inside. That was my immediate reaction to being in public. People's eyes looked blank. Their faces were haggard and expressionless like zombies.

I wanted to stand up on the train and do that thing that I hate when other people do it: start preaching out loud. I desperately wanted to stand up and shout: "Wake up and live people! Celebrate your life!" But I knew that I was just temporarily delusional and that it would take a few days for the standard New York City attitude, otherwise known as "indifference," to come over me. Then I would be normal and like the other New Yorkers again.

Leaving New York to go to Brazil was pretty scary at first. All of my friends and relatives said that I would be physically harmed or financially scammed in Brazil. Some of my friends said that they were going to call the US Embassy and have them get me out of Bahia when they hadn't heard from me for a few days. Boy, would I have been thoroughly pissed off at them. I was so fulfilled in Bahia that I didn't need to communicate with anybody on the outside, until I needed a money wire of course.

Once, from Bahia, I emailed some friends because I couldn't get in touch with my little brother, who was responsible for managing my money wires. Once they got my email they were comforted knowing that I was safe and not "missing." But then they were annoyed, and maybe even a little jealous, to find out that I needed money to **prolong** my stay in Bahia. My dear old friends were rather disappointed to learn that I was not being held at gun point against my will somewhere in the Amazon Jungle.

In Bahia, there were very few internet cafes, but it didn't even occur to me to email the people back home after I informed them that I was in Bahia. But I understand their side of this story because I was emailing them almost daily from Rio. My money situation while I was in Brazil was really "effed" up. It's a long story but here's the short of it:

About a month before I left for Brazil, I was referred to an accountant who offered all of his new clients a free review of their tax returns on the promise that he could find more tax return money, than his competitors already did for them. This accountant met all of his clients in his home office. He was a tall, dark and handsome Black man- married with two kids- living in a huge two family home in an upscale neighborhood where his was the only Black family on the block. This man introduced himself as a Reverend, said he used to preach on the pulpit and claimed to have a PhD.

Ok. Nice guy, nice house, nice family; I met his wife, kids, mother, maid and dog over the course of three visits before I gave him my tax records from the prior three years. This religious accountant amended my taxes for the past three years and promised me a total tax return of $5,000 in back taxes that I had overpaid according to his calculations. Sure, it sounded too good to be true but I figured it added up like that from the three years combined.

I had met a few of his other clients and they were talking about getting tax returns through his service in the amounts of ten to fifty thousand dollars after he amended their back taxes. The other clients were so impressed with the accountant that they were using his service to obtain no-money-down mortgage loans and using him to close on "straw man" property deals.

My problem was that the accountant promised me a rapid refund on the amended tax returns. He claimed that I would receive the return of about $5,000 before I left for Brazil. What really happened is that I used savings to buy my ticket to Brazil and cover my hotel stay for the first week then I had my little brother wiring me money as needed. All the while the accountant kept promising me that any day (during my stay in Brazil) he was going to deposit me a check for $5,000. I called and emailed this guy from Brazil so many times that I don't care to remember just how many times. He never did keep his word. He finally wired just $2,000 after I was three weeks into my trip.

When I got back to NYC I was furious with the accountant. What an asshole. I went to this house unannounced. There was a police car parked out front. I walked around towards the backyard and entered his house through the side door. People were arguing in the basement where his home office was. I stood still at the top of the basement stairs listening to their argument. Apparently, one of his customers had come over demanding a physical copy of the tax return statements that he submitted to the IRS on her behalf. The accountant refused to hand them over and when she refused to leave without her paperwork, he called the police. The police sided with the accountant and told the client to leave his house immediately.

Outside, in front of the accountant's home I spoke with the client. As it turned out the accountant was not an accountant at all. He was a scam artist who had defrauded many people. He filed false tax returns on our behalves and routed all of our tax return money into his personal bank account. Although I received $2,000 from his money wire, it would be all that I received. I was very, very lucky to have received that wire transfer from him at all. The good thing about the $2,000 coming so late is that it enabled me to pay my rent once I got back to NYC and have some pocket money as my savings were running low. My decision to prolong my stay in Brazil was largely based on the assumption that I was going to receive $5,000 cash any day while I was there.

I ended up having to pay back the IRS the total $5,000 plus penalties and interest even though the fraudulent accountant had pocketed most of that money. According to the IRS it was MY responsibility to choose an authentic accountant and verify their credentials. Therefore, it was my responsibility to pay it all back – and I did. But first I had to find a new job. That was the easy part.

I got hired by a non-profit organization to work with children. My job was to prevent children from becoming deviants. I created the exercises and activities that would teach the kids how to have self-confidence and work together through team building exercises. I enjoyed the job and got along really well with the kids and my colleagues. However, my supervisor was collecting a full-time check for less than part-time work. She was almost never present. I literally had to call her into the office (she lived within walking distance) whenever an auditor or inspector showed up at the job.

How does a Supervisor get away with not showing up to the job? That was easy, her mother sat at the head of the Board of Directors. It was the type of conflict of interest that gives all non-profit organizations a bad name. I didn't let any of that get to me. What eventually go to me was that when my supervisor finally did show up to work, she asked me repeatedly to falsify the data that she would report to the organization's funding sources. Being an absentee, she had not told anyone what the contract ordered us to do and she had no knowledge of what actually went on in her absence to use as a basis upon which to falsify the data herself. She didn't know any of the participant's names and the kids had no idea who she was, as head of the agency, either.

I refused to create the false numbers on several occasions and decided to instead write a detailed complaint outlining this attempt to deceive the funders to the agency's Board of Directors, NOT knowing that my supervisor's mother was at the head of the Board. Needless to say, the Board Director forwarded my complaint to her daughter, via email, and I was terminated soon after that without ever having received a response to my complaint from the Board.

I chose to not dispute this unfair termination just like I chose not to dispute the last one. Both terminations came on the heels of my written complaints, which I know are improper grounds for firing an employee. But if I disputed these firings with the Department of Labor and I won, I could potentially get those jobs back and I did not want to *have to* report back to those hell holes. I didn't want to fight for the opportunity to return to either hostile work environment.

Being unemployed for the second time, did not freak me out. I made the decision to downgrade my life style by moving into a smaller and cheaper apartment. I got rid of my television, since I couldn't afford cable anymore, and worked around the clock on building up my clothing line. I expanded my clothing line to include crochet hats and scarves as well as crystal jewelry that I handmade. I launched a website and rented booths at the downtown Brooklyn festivals where I sold my wearable art and distributed over 5,000 business cards.

Street vending was both financially and physically taxing and without a consistent source of income I found myself behind on bills in no time. My friend Sekhmet who had referred me to Sunset's prayer circle meditation a couple of years ago, was now encouraging me to try out a 3 day seminar that he had just completed. Sekhmet had been the bearer of good news for as long as I had known him. First he told me about the prayer circle then he taught me about the importance of water filters and nutritious supplements. So now that he was suggesting this seminar thingy I was pretty open to it seeing what it was all about.

At first, Sekhmet invited me to an introduction at the center where he took the seminar. I went to the free introduction because I trusted Sekhmet but I left it early feeling skeptical about what the seminar was offering. They said weird things in the introduction that I found highly annoying like: "the past has nothing to do with your future" and "you can have anything that you want" if you participate in their courses. I couldn't leave the free Introduction fast enough.

Even though I'd left in a disagreeable huff, the introduction staff would call me repeatedly until I broke down and wrote a letter to the seminar's Center Manager. I didn't keep a copy of the letter but I recall that it was not exactly friendly. I sarcastically implied that if their course was so damned good that they should give it to me for free instead of trying to harass me into it because life was hard enough and I could use a "breakthrough" right about now.

Instead of responding in kind to my sarcastic rant, the Seminar Leader mailed me a package that said "Congratulations! You have been officially registered for the upcoming course!" Without stooping down to my skeptical level, they honored my request. I was enlivened, the course truly started for me at the very moment that my "registration" was confirmed. Immediately, I felt a shift occurring inside of me. I felt optimistic for the first time in a long time, as if good things were coming my way.

I was in my upper twenties when I did the seminar. At the free introduction a few weeks prior to the seminar, I was prompted to list the areas of my life that I wanted to work on in the seminar. My list was pretty basic, I wanted to expand my clothing line and have a romantic relationship. If the course was promising to deliver results, then I wanted the results to show up in very *specific* areas of my life.

On the first day of the seminar I was surprised to find that there were well over 100 people in my course. 10 minutes early, I took a seat and committed to not socializing with anyone, no matter what. Then the person sitting in front of me, a brown skinned female with natural hair turned around and said to me, "Hey Ayana, good to see you!" It took me a minute to recognize her but it was Toni Blackman the community activist and rapper. She said, "I still wear one of your designs, the dress that I bought from you at the Street Festival." Ok, that's where I knew her from. Seeing Toni there in the course with me, put me at ease and gave me the ability to let my guard down. The course leader discouraged people who knew each other from sitting together so after our first break, I did not see Toni in the course again.

My course leader was a beautiful French woman with the stereotypical stuck-up French demeanor. I've been to Paris, France and they do live up to their anti-social-towards-outsiders hype. On the first day of the course, I decided to share. I went up to the microphone in front of all those people and talked about how I was sad that I never got to have a relationship with my deceased brother. Then I started crying.

The facilitator just looked at me as if she were annoyed and said in her most rude French accent "You don't get it, go sit down!" I was too shocked to be embarrassed as I headed back to my seat. I thought to myself what a witch this facilitator was. But by the last day I thought differently of her, at the end of the course I said to myself "Aaahhh, but she is a good witch!"

The course did not directly address the areas of my life that I written about in the free introduction: business and romance. Instead I learned, much to my surprise that I was a self-absorbed jerk and the judge, jury and executioner of everyone in my life. I had to come to grips with the fact that I was a stage four "clinger." In communication I would cling on to my point of view and that would lead to clinging on to people until I felt that they understood or (more importantly) agreed with my point of view. Even in death I was still judging my brother (and grandmother) based on my point of view that they didn't care for me while they were alive. They were just two more people in my collection of those who had abandoned me. In order to prevent myself from being abandoned again I had been relating to people from the point of view of "I have to abandon you, before you abandon me."

Learning these about myself things helped me to understand why I wasn't feeling very creative or romantic at that point in my life. I had more complaints about life than solutions and my communication with others was always littered with skepticism. My biggest breakthrough came from an assignment that I thought was going to be impossible to carry out with integrity.

The course leader instructed everyone to call their parents and "get complete" with them by apologizing for being a brat. At the first break I went up to the course leader and told her without blinking, "that assignment is appropriate for all of these people who were raised by their parents. They have no reason to be upset but *I was abandoned*! Why should I have to call my parents and apologize to them? They should be calling me!" Again, the course leader didn't give me the time of day. She gave me a pretty stern look and I just felt like a brat. All I could do was walk away.

On the break I took my cell phone out and looked at it, just the thought of calling either my mother or father brought up a huge lump in my throat. They had never apologized to *me*. I had no compassion for my own parents who had the same issues as some of the patients that I worked with as a Mental Health and Substance Abuse counselor. It always bothered me that I had so much compassion for the patients that I worked with but none for own my parents. It would require loads of compassion for me to complete the assignment. I didn't want to do it. Regardless, I found a quiet place to sit in front of a municipal building far up the steps and off to the side where I could cry, unnoticed, at a safe distance from the general public on the sidewalk.

I called my mom first because she was in a mental hospital again. My mother had a long history of battling bi-polar and schizo-affective disorders. As a child I'd seen my mother chop all of her long dreadlocks off, throw household items out of our fifth floor apartment window and walk around outside naked leaving us, her children unattended in the apartment. The mental illnesses had surfaced when she was a teenager and were brought on by the death of her father, according to multiple family accounts. All of these horrible images came to mind whenever I spoke to my mother. Her illness is degenerative and she has been going in and out of mental hospitals, like a revolving door, several times per year since I was 12 years old.

There was a time when my mother was sentenced to jail for 5 years but at least she wrote letters during that period. It was I who gave up on our relationship at some point. There was one too many mental hospital visits where I saw my mother looking really bad and one day it drove me away from her. The patients around her looked even worse off than she was. It was the kind of scene that horror movies are made of. The mental wards in NYC look like prisons. There are a lot of locked doors you have to go through to get in and out when visiting those places. I would go in with a brave face on and visit with my mother while all of these random people with varying mental disorders, and body odors paced back and forth while talking to themselves, or doing something worse than that to themselves. Once all of the doors were locked behind me and I got in the elevator on my way to the hospital exit, I would have my own emotional breakdown. Only then would the tears flow. I felt guilty for having to leave her there, in a filthy prison with other unrestrained mental patients.

The stories she told me about some of these places didn't help either. She said that she had woken up on one occasion, covered in shredded paper, to find her roommate striking matches onto her bed. There was nothing I could do about it, I was a minor, but she still sent me on plenty of wild goose chases hunting down adults for money that she was owed. She was very demanding and made it my responsibility to pick up her broken pieces on the outside world while she was locked away.

I wished I could take my mother out of those places with all of those random people, some of whom had undoubtedly been picked up off the NYC subways. But who am I to judge? My mother has admitted to panhandling on and sleeping on the subways herself during bouts of homelessness. The most I could do to help her in my teenage years was to bring her some canned food s that I would steal from the pantry of my group home. I would pack a weekend bag to go visit her with no clothes in it, just canned and dry foods and sometimes frozen meats. All of these things came to mind as I sat on the steps of the municipal building looking at my cell phone with tears streaming down my face. I decided to make the call. She answered the phone.

"Hi mom, how are you?"

"Hi Yani, I'm still in the hospital. I'm so frustrated that I can't do anything right."

"Well Ma, I'm in a course this weekend and it's going well. I wanted to call you to clear some things up. I know that I don't call often and I haven't visited you in years (the tears welled up again) but it's not because I don't care. (My voice cracked) I have been your judge, jury and executioner for several years now ever since we went into the Foster Care system and I want you to know that I am going to stop judging you now and just be a daughter and let you be my mother."

I could tell that she was teary when she replied "I'm so happy to hear you say that, I love you and I am very proud of you. Hearing you say that makes me want to live again."

"I know mom, but I have to go I will call you later. I love you."

I was so choked up that I couldn't speak and I didn't even know what to say next. I just didn't want the conversation to degenerate into an argument. I called my father next to see if I could duplicate those results. My father's excuse for abandoning his three kids is that he had been on hard drugs like heroin, coke and crack for the past 20 years or more. My parents sold drugs out of our apartment (before I went into foster care around age 4) so there had been a lot of foot traffic in and out of our home- drug addicted customers and police of various sorts included. Let's just say that the cops didn't always make an arrest yet they never left empty-handed. I believe that police unit went down in tabloid newspaper history as the "Dirty Thirty."

Considering the length of my father's drug abuse (my mom denies ever using drugs) I'm lucky to have been born with all of my fingers and toes. My father is in recovery for his drug addiction but he is still at the level of denial about the fact that he used to punch my mother around, which I saw and overheard on more than one occasion as a very young child. The last time I saw him was when I returned from Brazil. I went to visit him and give him a few souvenirs but we ended up getting into a fight that was so big that my father started chasing me down the street swinging on me until the police were called. My father wanted to take me to dinner with friends of his whom I'd never met whereas I just wanted to see him and his side of the family that day. He ignored my request to go to his mother's house and instead started driving me to his friends' house.

I lived two hours away from my father and his side of the family so I knew that if I went to dinner with his friends, it would make him look good but I would not get to see his mother and aunt. As he was driving I asked him to take me to either his mother's or aunt's house and then go to dinner with his friends since that was so important to him. He turned to me and shouted, "I'm not your fucking chauffer you dumbass bitch, that's why you got stranded in Brazil!"

Well, well, well. I had to teach this man a lesson: *The buck stops here. I am NOT my mother and he will not attempt or succeed at putting any fear in my heart*, I thought to myself. I looked at him and shouted right back, "I know you're not a chauffeur, you're a fucking piece of shit loser and you still have a crack head mentality!" He got the memo, made a U-turn and drove me to his aunt's house where we both got out of the car and threw our hands up like two professional boxers...

With all of these chaotic thoughts running through my mind, as I sat near the top of the staircase of the municipal building, I went ahead and called my father - he too answered his phone.

"Hi... Dad?" That was a breakthrough in itself I never called him "dad." I had been calling him "father" for as long as I could remember.

"Yes! Hey Yani how's it going?

"Um, it's going good, I am doing this seminar thing and I wanted to call you and clear the air..."

"OK, well I'm all ears," he said.

"You know how when we speak I am like, always talking to you through clenched teeth? Um, I've been holding a grudge against you for so many years. I am going to stop judging you and just be your daughter and let you be the parent from now on."

"Well, ok my daughter! That sounds great! Reminds of something I heard in an NA meeting, but no matter. I know you've been talking about going to grad school lately and whenever you finish let me know where to send the money so I can help you pay off your student loan."

"Ok Dad, thank you, that's great. My break is almost over. I'll talk to you later."

I was on an emotional high and an unbelievable roll. I wanted to call one more person to see if I could cause another major breakthrough before my little 30 minute break was up. I called my ex-fiancé, the one who had cheated on me during the course of what I thought had been a perfect relationship. Ever since we had broken up, years before I did the seminar, we still remained friends. But sometimes I would awkwardly drunk dial him and ask "Do you still love me?" And he would say "Yes and do you still love me?" and I would say "No."

It was now clear to me that I had been keeping him as a friend just so I could keep rubbing his mistakes in his face and the poor guy was sticking around for it. I was feeling really good after speaking to my parents and wanted to keep the good times rolling, so I went ahead and called him.

"Hey Pootie, what's up?"

"Ay-a-na" he said in a sing-songy voice, "what are you up to? You've always got something interesting going on."

"Well Pootie, I am in a weekend seminar type of thing and I really like it. I have something to clean up with you now that I've learned more about myself. Basically, I couldn't forgive you for cheating on me and even though we stayed friends I never really did forgive you but I do forgive you now and there's something I want to tell you... I kinda understand why you cheated on me. I was emotionally unavailable and impossible to satisfy. There were times that you tried to get through to me and I would shut you down by being argumentative. You were good to me and I enjoyed our relationship but my mentality was that I had to abandon you before you abandoned me. And so I've got to tell you something that I kept from you during our relationship... I cheated on you first, a year before I caught you cheating. I never cheated a second time but I just didn't say anything about the one time that I did. I cheated on you with a colleague too. It's funny that a year later you did the same thing to me."

He took the news pretty well and asked why I had cheated in the first place had asked him repeatedly reminded him that sh to me, he told me "If a man ever cheats on you, you should break up with him." I made a mental note that he must have intended to cheat on me at some point in the future because who in their right mind would warn their fiancée about her dating future?

I told him that I interpreted his saying that to me as his saying: *one day I am going to cheat on you and when I do it will mean that our relationship is not salvageable so you should break up with me.* He said that I should have forgiven him sooner and stayed with him instead of breaking up since I had cheated first. But I told him that I could only trust myself at that point. I knew that I would never cheat on him again but I could not rest easily on the assumption that he would never cheat on me again. My cheating was a pre-emptive strike. I had no idea what his cheating was really based on, at the root of it. I also told him that it was revealed in my meditation at Sunset's place that our relationship could not be repaired and how I had spiritually blossomed after we broke up.

I never would have attended that meditation or rekindled my relationship with God, had Pootie and I stayed together. And when we were together I loved him way above anyone else. As a young woman in love, I idolized my fiancé, he was my ₁/₂ worshipped him with my heart and no one much as I poured all of my love into ˑˡˡ of my hate into him as well. I was frequently inconsolable. He dealt with a lot of verbal warfare from me and was always really calm and gracious with me. He would listen to everything I said and then walk away.

Later on he would say "I deserved that." No matter how many times I apologized for spazzing out on him, I would find myself doing it again and again. I imagine that he felt sorry for me; my yelling at him usually ended in my bursting into tears from the exhaustion of yelling at the top of my lungs. Then I would have to apologize to him for my behavior. Then I would start brewing again because he was off the hook. None of the problems were ever resolved.

I admitted to starting arguments with him, when we were a couple, as a method of sending him away whenever he would drop me off at my grandma's family gatherings. I would become increasingly disagreeable the closer we got to my grandma's place in Harlem. All of my mother's generation of siblings battled with histories of substance abuse and/or mental illness, with the exception of one – who never did drugs but was born with a mental impairment. I didn't grow up with them and they haven't aged well.

Even though my relatives had funny nicknames like "Ham" and "Hollenjack" (as in "hollering Jack") I was embarrassed by my biological family on the few occasions that I did visit them. I would go so far as to pick fights with my fiancé to prevent him from meeting my family. I don't think he ever met any of my relatives face to face. He may have spoken to my mother over the phone once or twice when we were together but that's as far it went.

After all that drama, this was my chance to complete our past. I acknowledged him for the good times. He had been a very generous lover and a fun partner. We were always going to live concerts and Broadway shows. He encouraged me to launch my clothing line on the internet years before I would actually do it. When I casually said that I wanted to play the guitar one day, he bought an acoustic guitar, hand painted it and presented it to me along with the paid registration for a semester of "Guitar Playing 101" classes at the local college, Medgar Evers. He was the definition of a man: a provider, a protector and he made several attempts to include me in his immediate family.

I don't think I ever told him this, but one my fondest memories with him, was teaching him how to crochet. At first I was joking around with him so I picked up a little piece of yarn that had fallen on the floor and I gave it to him saying, "Here, I made you a hat." He took the 2 inch scrap of yarn out of my hand and put it on top of his head and with a big smile he said "Aw, thank you!" Then I couldn't stop laughing as he paraded around our apartment with that little scrap of yarn on top of his head until it fell off. A few times after that I would place scraps of yarn on his head when he wasn't looking, then I would laugh hysterically, like a hyena, at him until he figured it out.

What started off as a silly joke prompted me to want to teach him to crochet, at first he was resistant, but then he REALLY got the hang of it. I mean his color coordination and his way of creating random patterns with different yarn colors was really fashion forward. I sold a lot of hats that he crocheted and would give him the money when he'd come to break down my booths and take me home after festivals.

***

Participating in the weekend long seminar opened my eyes to the hidden agenda I was operating with in relation to people outside of my circle of loved ones as well. If you were my friend at that time, it wasn't because I was into you, but because I wanted *you* to agree with **me**. If folks didn't at least pretend to understand me or agree with my point of view which always boiled down to some version of "I'm right, right?" then the conversation was not over until I would say it's over.

If you would try to put your foot down by saying to me that the conversation was over (my gay male ex-friend tried it) that only led to phone calls, emails, long versions of "we need to talk" and of course nit-picky text messaging... Although it was all on my terms, I became even more irritated and irrational when people were not responding to me within the timeframe that I wanted them to or in the manner that I wanted them to, or in the language that I wanted them to. I didn't realize that I was being a control freak and an adult brat.

Every negative word I spoke shot from my lips like a bullet that travelled outward but still left a hole inside me. I had to be willing to accept that there was anger inside of me flying out in the form of violent words. I have never enjoyed witnessing fist fights, boxing or anything of that sort. Seeing people hit each other made me sick to my stomach ever since I was little and my father used to literally punch my mother around. But I have always sort of prided myself on using words to beat people up and leave people feeling *terrible* based on the things that I would say to them that I secretly hoped would haunt them for a long time to come.

As I became increasingly more sophisticated in spraying bullets with my words, so too did the gap inside of me grow larger, with each incident and the mental playback of each episode. I always felt guilty afterwards. I justified my behavior with the rationalization that other people were making me angry, they were pushing my buttons and so they earned my venomous bite. I was not aware that by lashing out, it was I who was taking the poison. The concept that I had adopted of "you are making me this way, it's your fault that I am forced to do the wrong thing," first showed up in my life at a very young age.

Probably around the age of six years old, while on a weekend home visit, I took some of my grandmother's makeup and put it in my tiny, little pants pocket. When she called us to lunch, I sat down at the table and her makeup slipped out of my pocket and fell to the floor. My grandmother didn't overreact in front of me. She just looked at me and said "You're stealing, that's not a good, you don't steal from family. You steal from strangers." Obviously I was trying to hide it from her by having it in my pocket and not saying anything about the fact that I had taken it from her bedroom.

A few years later when I was about 10 or 11 years old, I would continue spending weekends at my grandmother's place where one of my aunt's and a cousin also lived. On one of these visits my aunt said that one of her diamond rings had gone missing. Grandma immediately blamed it on me and said that I couldn't go any further into their home than the living room, kitchen and bathroom in their rail road apartment. All of the bedrooms were in the back of the apartment.

Now, you have to understand that in the bed rooms there were *beds,* cable television, video games - all of the fun and entertainment was in the bedrooms. In the living room, all of the furniture was pea green, preserved from the seventies and covered in plastic. I'd now have to sleep on that. The TV was a 26 inch black and white old time model. The only shows that were worth watching on the TV in the living room were "The Twilight Zone," "I Love Lucy," and the "Honeymooners." I'd rather watch cartoons in color TV with my cousin in her room or watch movies with people cursing in them on cable TV in my aunt's room.

Since I was sectioned and cordoned off to the living room I was not able to enjoy the time that I spent there anymore. On top of that my grandmother was directly communicating with my Foster mother and telling her that I was a thief. I stopped going to visit my grandmother but my Foster mother was still telling me that I was a thief and so eventually, I became a thief. I started going into the piggy bank on her dresser and shaking whatever change I could get out of it: quarters, nickels, pennies whatever I could finagle out of that thing. I took a butter knife and pried the edge of the coin slot open and then the coins just slipped out into my hand. I used those coins to buy candy before and after school.

I would the eat candy to feel better. I would eat loads of candy to fill the gap inside of me and then eat more as a reward for being "brave" and standing up for myself by stealing the change. It was like doing a ritualistic victory dance at a party with no friends. I felt very lonely.

It didn't even console me when a few months later, my grandmother called my foster mother to tell us that my aunt had found her missing diamond ring in a shoe box under her dresser. My grandmother was crying and calling on the Lord saying that all along she knew that I didn't steal the ring.

Twenty years later, grandma passed away and I did not attend the funeral, but not because of an isolated incident. The deeper heart break for me was the fact that my grandmother had 6 kids of her own and about 14 grandkids from them. For some reason, my grandmother took in all of her kids and their kids and their kids whenever they were down and out dealing with poverty, drug addictions and imprisonments – with the exception of my mother and her three kids with my father. My grandma took my older sister and raised her on behalf of my mother, but my grandma made no such offer (to my knowledge) to care for me, my older brother (R.I.P.) or my younger brother.

It's so embarrassing that out of my whole biological family only the three of us (me and two brothers) went into the foster care system. My grandmother was the matriarch of our family. All of the major holidays were celebrated at her house. My grandmother always had enough fried chicken, white rice and cabbage on hand to feed everyone who came through her door, whether they were announced or unannounced. Grandma always had enough slippers and housecoats to go around. She always made a way to accommodate everyone that spent the night and always served them a continental breakfast in the morning. Grandma's fridge was an open door but you'd better not touch her Pepsi unless you wanted to meet Jesus that day.

As much as I loved my grandmother, I held an ever increasing grudge against her, in my heart, for as long as she was alive. I was very aware of the difference between my father's children and the entirety of my mother's side of the family. We were outsiders but I was the most sensitive to it. My younger brother was unaware of this and strangely my older brother was sort of a pet to my grandmother. He was without a doubt her second favorite grandkid. But she didn't take him out of foster care either.

I would cringe as my brother and grandmother would call each other pet names, and smooch on the lips whenever they greeted each other. I am convinced that they are even united in heaven together now. When I try to talk to one of them at night in my prayers, I can't imagine either of them up in heaven alone. In my mind, they are hugged up together as angels in heaven. This is how connected they were on Earth.

I didn't assign them to heaven, in my mind, because of any altruistic endeavors from their humanly lives. Neither of them cared for me as much as I did for them or at least they never did show it. But the bottom line for me is that I don't believe that there is a hell in the afterlife. I can't tell you to go to hell if I don't believe it exists. The descriptions of a burning hell are works of fiction written by some of the best authors in history.

Hell, in my honest opinion, is any distraction that takes me off of my path, which is to heal. When I stop healing, I am in hell. You can heal or you can go to hell. It's like hell on Earth when everything's going wrong and life is in total breakdown. Also, the negative side effects of not healing are basically allowing the painful symptoms to grow and worsen over time.

I know that I need my brother and grandmother to support me from the other side and I believe that they do. Shortly after my brother's death in his mid-twenties, I was lost. We never connected in this life. We didn't grow up together and the only hope I had for us to have a relationship was that one day when we were in our THIRTIES we would connect and make up for lost time.

But that would never happen and so his passing away at such a young age was tragic and it totally devastated me. I seemed to be the only person crying at my brother's funeral, the others all but expected him to die at a young age. I kept asking my mother: Did Idris love me? I had honestly never once heard him say "I love you" to me. The one time I asked my older brother if he loved me he just said to me, "Can horses run?" But my brother showed up for me after his untimely death in an even greater way than he did in his short life.

My meditation with Sunset took place one year and three months before Idris passed away. In that meditation I asked spirit what I needed to do to get right with my life. In response, I had a vision of me with my father and my two brothers all seated and holding hands around a dinner table. It was an image of us all in our present day form as adults at that moment in time. Three months after that meditation with Sunset, my father came up with the idea to take me and my two brothers out to dinner for each of our birthdays so each one would be a group celebration. We had never done that before.

As planned for that year me, my brothers, father and my father's mother dined together on each of the siblings' birthdays and at the end of that very same year my older brother's life came to an end.

About two weeks after the funeral I had an extremely vivid dream. I dreamt that I was at my mother's house with my little brother and everything around us was all white. The window was open and it was bright and sunny outside. The curtains were white and flowing. We were sitting on my mom's bed on top of a fluffy white comforter and my older brother appeared in front of us: myself, my mother and my little brother. My mother said to me in this dream, "Look Yani, Idris is dead but he is here with us now!" I jumped all over him with hugs and kisses and told him I missed him. He told me that he loved me.

As the dream continued, he whipped out a guitar, literally out of thin air, and he proceeded to play a Bob Marley song from it. The entire song "Three Little Birds" was streaming from his guitar as if his guitar was a radio. ALL of the sounds from the original song including all of the vocals by Bob Marley, the Wailers, and the I Three, plus each of the band instruments behind them - all of this music was coming out of his guitar. The last time my older brother and I sat around listening to Bob Marley with my Rastafarian mother was when we were 5 and 4 years old in real life.

But this was just a dream and in it I said to my older brother, as he played this reggae symphony out if his guitar, "Wow, how can you do that?" to which he replied, "I can do a lot of things now!" We all laughed out loud in unison, like the ending scene of a sitcom and the dream came to a close.

Back to life in the waking world, I interpreted the dream as a sign from my brother letting me know that he is in a better place now where he is limitless. The song "Three Little Birds" is very symbolic also because there were three of us that Idris was playing the song for: my mom, little brother and myself. The lyrics of that song are very simple and we grew up listening to that song. I was at peace with his passing immediately after that dream and now I imagine that my older brother is watching over and protecting me.

***

The seminar leader was on point when she told me to sit down after I cried on the microphone in front of 150 people about losing my older brother before we had a chance to build a familial relationship. How could she have known that I was making a pathetic attempt to get attention before I even knew that was what I was doing?

I even tried it again. At another point in the course I stood up and went to the mic, this time to ask the French witch a question. I said to her "Is it really possible to be complete with EVERYONE in my life? Because some people make me sick to my stomach when I think about them or when I am around them. Maybe I don't *need* those people."

And in her best French accent combined with a "ain't nobody got time for that!" attitude she said to me in response "It is your RESISTANCE to being with people that is making you sick!" I knew it was time to go and sit back down again, this time for the rest of the course. But I remained at the edge of my seat absorbing as many tools as I could. The seminar leaders forbade anyone from taking notes, it was a distraction that would prevent us from focusing and I don't doubt that people have taken the course for the purpose of knocking it off at a later date.

I think the wisdom presented in the course is so PRICELESS that it should be made for public television. Many of their distinctions were drawn directly from popular existential philosophers, and the words used so frequently in the course like: transformation, authenticity and being present were lifted from Zen Buddhism and mystics like Osho. Most important in my seminar experience was learning that the autopilot feature of negative thinking that human beings are born with is just a primitive neurological function that can be overcome.

The seminar was like a montage of the most effective strategies presented over the past century for reprogramming the mind. Once you reprogram your mind you are no longer physiologically impacted by negative memories. You still have your memories but you don't have the knee-jerk, hair trigger reactions to them like you used to. People in your life no longer have to walk on egg shells around your "issues from childhood" because you no longer wear your problems on your sleeve.

The road to overcoming negative thinking is not easy because it requires patience, effort and compassion for yourself and others simultaneously. Usually we only have compassion for one person at a time and depending on the circumstances we take our pick. Transforming one's reliance on automatic thoughts is akin to destroying one's ego. The ego may never be fully destroyed but it can be "re-programmed" for evolutionary purposes, if you are into that kind of thing. I happen to be very into the evolution of the human race. It is calling me forward. I believe that the type of information presented in the seminar could have the potential of bringing peace on Earth. After I completed the exercise by calling my mother, father and ex-fiancé I felt whole, complete and perfect, like I never needed to read another self-help book again!

Chapter 8: Life Goes On

Through the rest of my twenties, I did my best to apply all of the tools that I had picked up from the seminar. Life became more fluid and I was able to get a lot of things accomplished in a short amount of time. While working a full-time Counseling job, I enrolled in an accelerated MBA program. And I continued to travel. As if school and work were not enough to keep me busy, I decided to take a week long vacation to Jamaica during the Easter break. With my Rastafarian background and long, brown dreadlocks, I fit in just perfectly there.

The funny thing was that I couldn't understand a word that people were speaking to me. Surely, they were speaking English but the accent was too thick for me to understand. It felt like I was being so rude by constantly having to say "huh?" and "what?" every other second. In Jamaica just like in Brazil, people were naturally attracted to me and took me to all kinds of events like *passa passa* where I danced along with what seemed like a thousand people, to dance hall music in a massive, open field at night.

Everything was going fine until I saw a military tank roll through. It crept up so slowly that I didn't even see it in the dark until the crowd parted in front of me like the Red Sea. Then I saw the tank, even though it was dark. There was a man in a military uniform hanging out of the top of the rolling tank and he had a large rifle in his hand as if to say to the crowd *"If ANYBODY is going to be doing ANY shooting out here tonight, they are going to have to deal with us!"*

The atmosphere was so festive that even the tank occasionally rolling through didn't disturb the party. There were carts that sold freshly grilled jerk meats, roasted corn, sodas and beer. I had been warned by one of my classmates/Caribbean friend, Ryan, before I left for Jamaica that I should attend at least one *passa passa* but that I should NOT wear a short skirt to it. Dancing in the middle of that field in real time, I understood why he'd given that advice. Apparently, there are camera crews that go to all of the *passa passas* and follow the girls around. Some girls do choreographed routines for the camera crews but what makes people buy videos of these particular Jamaican dance parties, off the streets of Brooklyn, NY where I live is that the cameras often end up UNDER the dancing girls' skirts. Just as I moved along with the crowd out of the way of the rolling tank, I made sure to avoid the aggressively roving camera crews.

Jamaica was an amazing place to vacation. I spent a couple of days in Ocho Rios then I spent the rest of my stay in Montego Bay. I rented an apartment from a Rasta family, who built the house I where I stayed in Catherine Hall. I was a short cab ride away from the beach, mall and clubs. At the Aqua Sol beach I went snorkeling for the first time in my life. The beach was almost completely empty except on the holiday. Most days, I felt like I owned that beach.

The nightclubs in Montego Bay get packed really quickly. The locals go to clubs to see the acts just as much as the tourists do. I saw far more locals than tourists in the tourist area clubs. I suppose Easter is a good time of year to see Jamaica if you really want to have a lot of space from other tourists everywhere except the clubs. My guide insisted on taking me to a club one night, I couldn't refuse. There was a full-out concert but I am not familiar with contemporary dancehall artists.

When I got back to NYC and told my Caribbean friend, Ryan, about the concert I attended in Montego Bay he asked me who performed. The only name I could remember seeing out of so many live acts was Busy Signal. I remembered that performer because he actually used the busy signal sound in his set. Ryan kinda went beserk on me. He was all excited like "you don't know who Busy Signal is?" This guy is an international reggae artist, very popular among the Caribbean populations in Brooklyn where I live even though he is from Jamaica.

Jamaica was a really good trip for me. I got to hang out on the beach, visit the country side, caves and take in a lot of the local culture. I took lots of pictures. Jamaica is so GREEN that some of my nature pictures look photo-shopped. Since I was travelling alone, I didn't make it Kingston where every Jamaican in my Brooklyn neighborhood claims to have come from.

At the end of the school year, it was a mandatory part of the curriculum to study abroad. My entire class went to London for one week and Paris for another week. It happened to be London's marketing version of "Black Friday" when we were there. I got to know Selfridges and Top Shop quite well during my stay. I had a MySpace friend that I met in real life in London, the fabulous make-up artist Rumel. She became my tour guide, shopping all day, clubbing all night. Rumi helped me to get into all of the trouble that my heart desired. She's a good friend to be from a social networking site.

I retuned the favor when Rumi visited Brooklyn, NY less than a year later in order to take advantage of OUR shopping discounts! The money exchange is not in our favor when shopping in the UK. So for a London lass like Rumi the cost of shopping in NYC is massively discounted. Not so much for me in the

UK however. Regardless, I had to FedEx two full boxes of merchandise, from my hotel in Amsterdam, back home to myself in the states because I had all but lost my mind buying clothes, shoes, and accessories primarily in Selfridges of London. My biggest splurge was this huge, metallic silver, leather Fendi bag. It became my school bag when we got back to the states.

My favorite things about Paris were the food, the hash and the free alcohol. At many traditional restaurants they have a way of slipping you a few drinks that never end up on the tab. I was seated at a nice restaurant and right away a glass of red wine was poured in front of me. The red wine was refilled twice after I "emptied" it. With dessert, a shot of liquor was given to me. This happened in a handful of traditional restaurants.

But on the streets, no one would talk to me if I didn't speak French. Only the people of "color" who spoke a bit of English would help me to get around Paris. My fondest memory of Paris, was Disney! I was a little old to be going to Disney for the first time but hey, I really enjoyed myself.

From Disney Paris, I have some of the oddest pictures that have ever been taken of me, but they capture my overwhelming excitement while I was on a couple of the rides. According to the photographic evidence, I pretty much lost my mind on the Haunted Elevator ride and it seems like I really thought that I was shooting real aliens on the Buzz Lightyear ride. Toy Story is one of my top faves... I didn't leave Disney Paris without waving good bye to Mickey and purchasing my very own pair of Mouse ears.

Speaking of "Mickey," that's the nick name I gave to my grad school buddy that went with me to Amsterdam when all of the other students went back to NYC with the teachers. About four of us classmates had planned to visit Amsterdam after Paris and London but only me and Mickey had the financial balls to go through with it. We stayed in a nice hotel right across the street from the train station that would take us back to the airport.

The problem with Amsterdam is that it seems to be composed ENTIRELY of tourists, none of whom speak English. Additionally, the locals DO speak English but with such a heavy accent and mixture of slang that I had no idea what they were talking about. In Jamaica and Amsterdam, the locals understood my "Neu Yawk" accent perfectly. However, it was I who had sudden bouts of deafness when trying to converse with them.

If it wasn't for my classmate Mickey I would never have found the post office in Amsterdam, they had a different word for it. But it took us so long to find the building that as we approached it, the entrance gate slowly shut down right in front of our eyes. My only option was to leave the boxes containing my London, Paris and Amsterdam souvenirs with the hotel staff and trust them to FedEx my stuff back to my Brooklyn address.

Aside from the language barrier, Amsterdam was pretty darn cool. I don't remember much about this three day trip, you can imagine why, but the food was amazing. Even the McDonalds was held to a higher standard of quality in Amsterdam than we see in NYC. Maybe just because it was Amsterdam they sold authentic round, Danish style apple pies, not the brick in a box we get in the states.

Mickey's fondest memory of Amsterdam was when we dropped mushrooms. I told Mickey a few lines that were inspired by the horror movie "Shrooms." I said to him, "Listen Mickey, I've done this before but you haven't. We are going to eat these shrooms at the hotel. We are not leaving the room at any time or for any reason until tomorrow morning. We will not be going outside for a walk after we take these. We will not call anyone for help after we take these... Do you understand me?"

He was looking me in the eyes, then he looked down and ripped the lid off his package of shrooms. Mickey wolfed down his whole box of mushrooms like it was his last meal. The box the shrooms came in was about the size of a package of tofu and it was really fresh, purchased from a refrigerated dispensary.

I ate about half of my box, since it was labeled "Full Body Experience." Mickey, if I remember correctly, ate the other half of my box too. We had cola, orange juice and food in the room with us to consume so that if a bad trip set in we could get off it quickly. Mickey had triple the quantity of my dose so he tripped out for several hours while I watched TV, bored out of my mind, nauseas, yawning and tearing up but not tripping out. Every so often I would ask Mickey to tell me about his trip so that I could have a little entertainment. Mickey thought he was at the club and he kept getting up and reenacting what he was seeing, much to my amusement.

Out of boredom, I finally said to Mickey about three or four hours after we had eaten the mushrooms, "Mickey I'm bored, let's go outside." He turned to me and in a very clear voice he said "NO, Ayana, we are NOT leaving this room, we are NOT going outside and we are NOT calling anybody. Do YOU understand me?"

Damn, he may have been tripping out but he was right.

***

Once I completed the MBA program, with a 3.7 GPA, I felt like I could do anything. My mother had been encouraging me to become a Marketing Executive ever since I was a little kid. Clearly, with an MBA degree and my BA in Psychology, it was now a very realistic possibility. However, I had another plan for myself. I saw myself taking the decade of experience I had in Counseling, Group Facilitation and the Arts and combining them with my credentials and contacts to start my own non-profit organization. The goal would be to teach teenagers how to use all types of media technology and then support them in creating positive images.

I was still working the same Counseling job after I graduated with my MBA that I had the whole time that I was a grad student but I was inspired about the possibility of quitting the job after I got my non-profit organization up and running which could take at the least, one year. After taking a series of grant writing courses at the New York Foundation Center, I was convinced that this was something I could take on. I had the necessary amount of professional contacts who were interested in staffing a small operation. I held conference meetings, created the name of the organization, drew up a proposal and initiated the paperwork process towards becoming an organization.

Then, out of the blue, my mother called me at work and told me that she had been diagnosed with breast cancer. She panicked and thought she was dying. My mother had been living in Connecticut for the past ten years at this point and I only visited her every other year. I avoided my mom like the plague because she was an instant and tireless critic. It also made me feel deeply saddened to see the impact of her degenerative mental condition but this was a serious matter. I took a 90 day (unpaid) leave of absence from work to spend time with my mother. If I remember it correctly, I stayed out of the office for more than the 90 days, I didn't return to work until she made a full recovery.

When I did return to work, my job was still there but so was my work load that should have been distributed among my colleagues. I was told by my Supervisors to back date and fill in about a dozen client forms that were overdue. They gave me a list of old dates that I was told to fill in on the cover pages of the overdue paper work. The problem was that I wasn't even in the state of New York, much less in the office during the dates that I was being told to fill in and sign my name next to. Furthermore, in order for this ruse to work, I would have to manipulate the clients into signing their names and forge the date (with a back date that met the deadline) next to their names, instead of letting them put the current date next to their names as they should have and normally would have.

I flatly refused to do it and told the supervisors that what they were asking me to do was unprofessional and unethical. In order to get the work done, I filled the forms in and put the *correct*, current dates on them and allowed the clients to sign and date them as normal without altering the truth. My supervisors were not amused and they wrote me up for submitting late documents as a formal disciplinary action, which I refused to sign and instead wrote a complaint to their superiors, who in turned called me in to the main office and fired me. It was my third termination and well, well, well, this brings us back to the beginning of this book... where it all began with ME getting fired – again.

The beginning of this book was not only my third time being fired from a job, it was also my third time being fired after writing a complaint. The first time I got fired was after I contacted OSHA to report a bathroom pipe that leaked for two days, from the ceiling over my office. The second time I was terminated came after I refused to cover for my supervisor's incompetence by falsifying the numbers that went to the funders. And finally, the third time I was let go was based on – what else? Once again, it was my refusal to falsify data.

It's unfortunate that social service agencies so often resort to defrauding their funders instead of providing the services that they are funded to. This is why it is advantageous for them to fire the complainer. For starters, there are more workers willing to forge the papers than to do the work of engaging their clients. Additionally, auditors tend to give the agencies a heads up warning before they inspect the files. If more auditing services conducted impromptu audits, then it would be obvious that paperwork was missing or going to be submitted late.

A technology based solution would be to have clients swipe their ID cards upon entrance and exit of their Counselors' offices, this way the service dates can't be hand forged and everybody involved would have to really, truly see each other face to face and actually provide some support services on a consistent basis. But that's not my problem anymore. Now I have to reinvent myself so that I can survive.

***

What am I going to do next? My problems now are hard to define. After so many years of working in hostile environments, I'd have to dig deep in order to center myself before taking another road. It's more of a feeling than a distinct thing. The only term that I can use to describe the discomfort that I have when I look within is an internal void. It feels like something is missing. I tried to fill myself by putting square pegs into round holes. In other words, my solutions were ill-fitted to the situations. Now, I need to draw on all of my knowledge, experience and faith in The Creator to understand what must be done to heal the holes. But what if each hole is REALLY an open **SPIRITUAL** wound?

Perhaps the hole growing inside of me that I was trying to fill, at *this* stage in life by eating is the mourning of my womb, a type of empty nest syndrome from the abortion that I had when I was 17 years old. Now I think that at 30-something years of age my desire to poke my nose into other people's business, care too much, tell them how to live their lives, become controlling or demanding too much attention from them is the energy I woulda, coulda, shoulda – but didn't - spend raising my own child.

Granted, I had interpreted a dream about the gospel choir presenting me with roses after my abortion at the age of 17 as a sign of forgiveness. I don't feel guilty about it but there was another dream I had a few days later. I saw myself walking down the street with a baby tiger. As we walked, it grew up a little bit and when I looked at it again I was holding hands with it and it was a little boy. I knew that this was my son showing himself to me from the spiritual realm. It was a very serene dream in which time had no meaning.

I now question if the dysfunctional behaviors and tendencies that I have acquired over the years has been karmic: the result of me aborting that life and then going forward, still feeling the sensations a mother has towards her child as the child would have grown up, wanting to have influence over him, guide him in the right way, give him the best life possible. I wonder if that's the void or the hole

I've been trying to fill all of these years later. Why else am I trying to give so much of myself to people who really don't want to be (s)mothered by me? This dysfunction has to have a root and I'm determined to find out what it is so that I can move on with my life.

So I was spending, or rather wasting, my life and time and energy and efforts with the best and greatest of intentions, on people and "relationships" who would prove my theory that I've been abandoned and left all alone. I would pour a lot of time and energy into listening to others and being a rock for them. I know how to be really present because I understand fear, loneliness and hesitancy about moving forward into the unknown. I became familiarized with these human psyche concepts through life experience, earning my BA in Psychology and years of professional training and experience as a Counselor. And so I would pride myself on being there for other people.

I'd be like, "yeah, I will be there with you to hold your hand in the dark so you won't feel alone." However I could not get that same type of attention, commitment or depth of presence from the people that I was putting my time and energy into. In this way, they would prove my theory that I'm abandoned and all alone. On a deeper level what was happening subconsciously, unintentionally was that I was attracted to people and situations that would result in my feeling abandoned.

Take for example, my relationship with a distant cousin. I didn't grow up with her nor did I get to know her until we were both adults. Upon first meeting, we looked the same on the outside. We both have dread locked hair styles, we both are into clothing design, crochet, jewelry making and painting. I made an instant decision to cling on to this relative for those reasons. But just a few hours into our first social gathering she unapologetically berated me over my political views. I wasn't even in a direct conversation with her when she interrupted and shut me down. Still, I humbled myself in her home, allowed it to happen and I justified it inside of my mind by writing her off as a bible thumper. Practically every conversation I had with her for the next 15 years went like that. I would share all of my dreams, goals and plans for my future with her and she would knock them down one by one in a hailstorm of judgment and criticism.

One day, after I listened to her criticize my whole life thus far and even the plans I had for my future, I told her that she was a hypocrite for missing the whole point of her own religion which is to NOT judge but to love others as much as she loved herself. After I explained that I had been on the receiving end of her constant condemnation for several years, she only said that I should have stopped her sooner. Then she abruptly ended our conversation and our relationship. A few weeks later I called her to see if we could talk it out but she flatly refused to talk to me.

I understand that she did not approve of my lifestyle but the truth was that I did not approve of her lifestyle either. Approval did not prevent me from accepting her unconditionally. But this was a relationship that I didn't need as much as I wanted it, the very first interaction I had with her was proof positive of that. Yet there I was 15 years later, realizing that it took me that long to figure out that I didn't need that relationship. I have to take responsibility for not being conscious and aware of the fact that it wasn't going to work out from the very first time that she berated and verbally abused me. Had I thought to myself back then, "Can I see myself tolerating this behavior from her 5 years from now?" I might not have spent so much time taking all that negativity in. It did nothing to decrease the inner void that was growing inside of me which was why I sought her out in the first place. It's not like she made any efforts to find me.

One day I turned the television on and caught an episode of Iyanla Vanzant's OWN Network show, *"Iyanla, Fix My life"* and I heard Iyanla say, "Vote for yourself!" I really liked that because I can see how easily people can literally become fervent over their political views but not so much over their own dreams. In my own life I had a whole lot of passion for endorsing other people and helping them complete, market and sell their projects but then not have that same level of intensity to vote for myself to be successful. I enjoy the process of being a stand for someone else's greatness even when they don't see it for themselves. However, I deserve to be just as happy and prosperous as I see it fit for my loved ones. I am turning my passions inwards nowadays as opposed to expending them outwards, towards other people's causes and agendas.

Perhaps my emptiness was coming from the realization that by this stage in my life, my 30's, that I should have a serious romantic relationship. Maybe the lack of close relationships and friendships that seem to be appropriate for this stage of my life were making me feel so empty. But I didn't want to force myself into a relationship just to fill a void that I was still trying to comprehend. Something had to change. I just didn't know exactly what yet.

In the midst of all of the confusion, I'd work up a pretty big appetite to fill the void. It was just another distraction. I rarely cooked yet I ate good. And by "good" I mean takeout, delivery and restaurant food. I managed to eat "good" by putting my meals on credit cards which is the living example of charging spiritual debt to a credit card. Although over eating expensive junk food was out of integrity with my health, wealth and morality meters, I was doing it so much that eventually, over the past 2 years, I gained 100 pounds over my lowest adult weight.

The awareness of my total weight gain was like hell on earth because it wasn't my first time being too overweight to enjoy my life. Gaining 100 pounds meant that I was 50 pounds heavier now than I was at a point in my life that I swore I'd never return to. That was literally half of my lifetime ago. I was a 228 pound teenager and I promised myself that would be my cut off point. I never thought I would be a 276 pound adult.

I started to examine my eating habits and patterns. There was a time when I was a health food enthusiast and lived on a strict vegan, vegetarian diet faithfully for at least seven years straight. I enjoyed exercising and had a bikini body which I proudly displayed on the beaches of Brazil, the Bahamas and Jamaica. One day, I decided that I was so healthy and in control of my diet that I could eat whatever I wanted to. Literally seven years later, I found myself 100 pounds heavier. It's hard to ignore 100 pounds so I let it motivate me to inquire within.

Once I created the intention to do so, I learned something about myself. In order to become objective, I split my awareness into two parts from only being the actor to also being the observer of my actions. I learned that I craved carbohydrates when I got stressed out. It came to the surface as I was learning to use a new computer program through online tutorials. I became increasingly frustrated. The more frustrated I became the more I wanted to chew on something. My jaws tensed, I could feel myself gnawing at the air and then I knew I was craving. The awareness of my cravings led me to explore them instead of immediately indulging them as I might normally do. I left my bedroom and approached my roommate; she was sitting on the floor of the living room hovering over her laptop.

I told her "I just realized that I crave carbs when I'm stressed out" and without looking she said to me, "Doesn't everyone?" I explained to her that I was craving pizza at the very moment of feeling stress. Being the free spirited, non-judgmental type of person that she is, she advised me to have the pizza if that was what it took for me to get over myself. I was pleased with her advice.

I was even grateful that she supported my choice to buy pizza. I told her I was going to order and asked her if she wanted to place an order with mine. She said that she didn't eat pizza so she passed on my offer. I was so glad that she passed. I didn't want her to see me eating it or rather, how much of it I could eat. In that moment I realized once again that I was simply craving the pizza as a way to manage my stress. I was really, really, *really* over thinking this pizza idea. Running the idea by my roommate gave me a moment to think about what I was going to do before I did it. So I thought instead of ordering pizza I would just eat some leftovers and then decide if I really wanted the pizza at a later time when I wasn't under any stress. The bottom line is that I did not order the pizza.

Chapter 9: From Spiritual Debt to Spiritual Power

Spiritual debt comes from lack of spiritual work and is something that cannot be charged to a credit card – not to yours or anyone else's, for that matter. We charge our spiritual needs to credit cards all the time, trading our souls in for "new stuff" like garments and gadgets. We do this on the promise of paying for it at a later date. But just like fiscal debt, spiritual debt does not disappear. It hangs in the balance, so to speak, like a bill that will soon be overdue. And just like some of us would rather die than confront our worst fears, I am sure that some of us would rather die than pay our debts - be they fiscal or spiritual. Spiritual debt must be paid through spiritual work. The good news is that there are multiple ways to do spiritual work.

There are other options to managing debt other than lying on it and then hiding from it. It is possible to transform your spiritual debt into spiritual POWER. From spiritual power comes the inspiration to resolve one's debts. The answers to spiritual questions do not come from the mind they come from the heart and soul.

The mind is an automatic tool, either you can use it or it will use you. I remember being a teenager, riding the bus after school. I noticed myself judging each passenger that boarded the bus. I was so deep into my negative thoughts that I could feel my face scrunching up and I could feel it so much that I had to stop myself. In that instant I thought to myself *well, maybe I should intentionally look for what's right, instead of always looking for what's wrong.*

That moment marked the beginning of my awareness of how to consciously use my mind as opposed to being on autopilot and allowing my mind to use me. Negative thinking occurs on autopilot. Defense mechanisms, reactions and overreactions occur on autopilot. It really takes some kind of conscious effort to distinguish yourself from the fleeting thoughts in your mind and create a new thought for yourself to build upon.

When mental autopilot takes over me, it really means that I've checked out, I'm not listening or being present to the environment surrounding me. Autopilot can take over so easily like when I am around someone who resembles someone else that I know. All that I can think about is the other person who isn't even physically there. Autopilot doesn't pay attention to what's happening in the moment so it renders us reactive instead of proactive. Autopilot is either self-critical or critical of others. It never says, "Go you! You can do it! This is your day!" You've got to say that to yourself because auto pilot is not who you are.

The only way to regain control over the internal auto-pilot is to practice the art of living moment by moment. Do whatever you are doing to the best of your ability and with mindfulness. That is how to show that you care. Take your time and pay attention to what you are doing. You might get it right the first time around. Being present to the moment you are in is the fastest way to shake off negative emotions that may arise from dwelling on the past or worrying about the future.

Sometimes, when I multi-task, I become accident prone. I tend to think about what I am going to do next while I am in the middle doing something already. On my way to the next task I may bump my hand or foot against a door frame because my eyes are not focused on the fact that I am in motion. I am not measuring the distance between my hand or foot and the door frame as I am running to complete my next thing to do if my mind's eye is pre-occupied with past or future based thoughts.

I always used to say that I was accident prone, now I recognize it as a (totally preventable) red flag, warning indicating that I need to slow down and focus on one thing at a time. Nowadays, when I catch myself moving too quickly, I say to myself out loud "How many things can I do at one time? One thing *but* I can do it very well." It's my little Mother Theresa meets Zen Buddhism remix. I have finally come to a place in my life where all of my spiritual lessons merge together seamlessly. There are numerous spiritual paths and I am convinced that there is something to be learned from each one of them. The more I can learn about spirituality, the more opportunities that I have to connect with God.

Spiritual work is like laundry, it's never done because there is always more to do. It's an ongoing process of learning about your own true nature. If you're not doing the work, you won't earn the benefit of your internal GPS providing CLEAR directions along your journey. Also, if you don't do your laundry, you won't have any (comfortable) clothes to wear.

Think back to a time when you procrastinated on doing your laundry and as a result had to wear ill fitting pajama bottoms, and no underwear, to the laundry mat. Now, *that's* an awkward walk. You feel naked, insecure and you wonder if people can easily see through your thin pants. Getting through life without spiritual guidance is an even more difficult walk. It's the equivalent of being "assed out."

If you fall off of your path and then choose to return to it, just like a GPS, the spirit - through intuition - will redirect your course and get you back on track. I don't drive but I've been a passenger on many car rides with people who continuously ignored the GPS automated lady telling them to make a turn. I'll cut them a sideways look like "You're going to ignore her again, *really*?", but ultimately the GPS doesn't complain out loud, so why should I? The GPS simply calculates a new route.

In life, intuition operates the same way, when you make a mistake God doesn't say anything (out loud) but when you seek His guidance and His wisdom no matter how far off course you've gone He will still work out a new route for you to continue your travels on.

Consider the term "painful memories." Do you have any? In this day and age we have an endless stream of methods to rid ourselves of painful memories. In this chapter I focus on the more healthy methods. I have been in therapy, seminars and in more churches than I can remember. Shortly after leaving these temporarily empowering, yet extremely gratifying mind-trips, I'd feel a decline in my ability to carry the euphoria forward. After a couple of days I'd be ready to bite somebody's head off again. Obviously, I need to take responsibility for transforming my anger instead of letting it consume my victim's head, just two days after the sermon is over.

This chapter is dedicated to the healing modalities that I have personally used to correct my course over the past 10 years. These quick tips and exercises were and still are helpful in times where I felt awkward, vulnerable, afraid and/or insecure. Any of these techniques may be used at any time for the purpose of healing yourself through your own inner compass. This list is not written in any particular order with the exception of "Relationship with God" being first. Overall, it's a list of ways to transform spiritual debt into spiritual power.

I'd love to get your feedback on spiritual practices that have worked for you. Feel free to email me at: info at ayanahinton dot com

Relationship with God

First and foremost, God has to be first in my life in order for it to work. I have attempted to stray away from God and I have learned that the QUALITY of my life is best when I am connected to God. When I find myself desiring someone or something I ask myself "Do you desire God as much as you do that man, those shoes or that junk food?" Put God first. The Bible says He will be ashamed of you if you are ashamed of Him.

Power of Prayer

A true seeker's intimate relationship with God begins with prayer. I talk to God all of the time now, not just when I am upset or in need of a favor. I have learned that God answers prayers and that He is always on time. I was only praying *when* I was upset. That's the only time I would ask for help otherwise I would think *I can do it on my own, I can handle it, I can take it on myself.*

Prayer is a constant state of communion and relationship not just for the purpose of getting what you want, but also for maintaining a state of grace and keeping a positive, empowering attitude about yourself. Potentially, the most important aspect of prayer is gratitude. Thank God and tell him how much you love him.

One day while in prayer I said to God, "I am so curious, will you show me your face?" And without a pause, God said to me "Look in the mirror." I burst out laughing. I know that I am communing with God when I am laughing while in a state of prayer or meditation because God is really funny.

Meditation

When I meditate, I remind myself to: Listen to God. Be still. Quiet your mind through focus. Focus your mind on breathing from your belly like a baby. Focus on your heartbeat. Feel the magic of your heart beat rocking your whole body. With your eyes closed, take the whole experience in through your inner eye.

Walking Meditation

If you really want to see the exact point where Heaven and Earth meet, I highly recommend that you visit a Botanical Garden. You may walk aimlessly and/or find a quiet place to sit. Take in all of the beauty around you. Quiet your mind by focusing on your breathing technique: from the belly. Allow nature to make love to your eyes.

It was in the Botanical Garden of Rio de Janeiro that I had a meditation which instructed me on how to heal my ear infection with the use of garlic.

Heart Point Meditation

The *Heart Point Meditation* is a technique that I created to heal myself when it's not possible to get closure from the other person. The other person may have already passed away or is just pretending to be dead in order to avoid you. We may never know if they received and read our emails or snail mails. This technique is good for bringing closure to situations without my having to SEE or HEAR the other person acknowledge my feelings.

In order to do the *Heart Point Meditation* you have to recall that meditation is about LISTENING:

1. Lay on your back, put your left hand on your heart. Breathe from the belly and be still until you can feel your heart beat pulsating throughout your body.

2. Now that you can feel how large your heart *really* is, acknowledge it for functioning, thank it for beating, for being love and for being the place where God lives inside of you.

3. Ask your heart to reveal to you what it will. *Prepare yourself to receive THE truth*. Be willing to see things that you don't want to see and to hear things that you don't want to hear. Truth does come from the heart. If you can be with what it says, you can heal the spiritual wound without having the physical presence of the other person there.

4. Once you have received the word, close the session by thanking your heart for doing its job so wonderfully, 24/7 and 365 days a year. Then, using your inner eye, envision each one of your other organs one at a time and thank and acknowledge them too. Notice the reactions of your internal organs to being acknowledged and appreciated. I felt MY heart pumping more forcefully, my lungs expanded immediately, my stomach

made noticeably audible digestion noises. And, I burst out with laughter.

In one of my *Heart Point Meditations* the word "free" came to mind. And my heart said to me "*I want you to know that this heart beats for all of the children in the world. I want them to be happy, healthy and well educated so that they can all be free. We adults have to take responsibility for sharing what we have with others so that we can all be free. Share what you have so that we can all have something.*"

Sometimes, I just listen to what my heart has to say. Other times I bring my troubles, my questions and my sorrows to my heart point meditation. One time I was conflicted about the extent of my responsibility to care for my immediate family. For many, many years -like more than half of my life - I have made a lot of sacrifices for them and it has been a burden. So I brought this issue to my *Heart Point Meditation*. And my heart said to me "*Do what you've been told. Do what you know to do. Self love, self preservation are your only responsibilities. Everyone is fine though they act like they are not. Heed your lessons. The purpose of life is to express yourself.*"

In previous meditations I had received guidance on how to heal from certain situations. I have to admit that I didn't always follow through on what those meditations had instructed me to do. For example, in one of my meditations I was instructed to stop drinking alcohol. But I did not follow through and there was a heavy consequence for that. I found myself in situations in which I could have been taken advantage of sexually or even worse, lost my life under the influence. It took me several years to really get the memo and apply it. Over the course of those years I lost a few wallets, vomited in public, verbally abused a few dates and Lord knows what else I can't remember because I had been drinking. Again, none of these things would have happened if I had listened to the advice given to me in my meditations.

So when my heart said to me in a state of meditation: *"Do what you've been told. Do what you know to do. Self- love and, self-preservation are your only responsibilities. Everyone is fine though they act like they are not. Heed your lessons, the purpose of life is to express yourself."* I knew what it meant.

Interpret Your Dreams

Sometimes I record my dreams in a bed side journal then interpret them when I wake up. One night I dreamt that I was at the airport with my suitcase trying to catch a flight, only to be denied because my passport had expired. When I woke up, I looked for my passport and learned that it was due to expire in 30 days. It showed me that dreams can have a powerful impact on your waking life, if you take a moment to reflect on them.

Understanding Generational Patterns

We have all heard the old Shakespeare quote "the sins of the father are to be laid upon the children." This type of expression shows up time and time again in so many different oral traditions. This rang true for me in a moment which enabled me to forgive my father for abandoning me into the Foster Care system. I had many layers of forgiveness to get through with my father before we could have a genuine relationship. This particular layer may well have represented most of the total thickness of the wall that I had built up between us.

One day I called my father, while he happened to be with his father on an eight hour drive, down south, to their family reunion. My father said that I was calling while they were in the middle of an argument. My father told me that this was the longest time in either one of their adult lives that they had spent together at one time. This long drive had brought up some painful memories for both of them.

My father said that he was upset that his father, my grandfather, had not been there for him after his parents divorced when he was about eight years old. I could not believe that MY father who had abandoned ME to the Foster Care system when I was just four years old had the audacity to complain to me about how his father had abandoned *him*. But I was also honored that my father was talking to me about his father while his father was sitting right next to him. This was an opportunity for me to understand the both of them a little bit better.

I asked to speak to my grandfather. I can count on one hand how many conversations I have had with my grandfather including this one but it didn't matter. My grandfather said that he was absent, when my father was a kid, because my grandfather worked two jobs to provide for them as his family. However, he said that he was mad at my father, his son, because by the time my grandfather was able to connect with my adult father, my father was hooked on hard drugs.

I was intuitively guided to ask my grandfather, "What happened to *your* father?" and my grandfather said that his father had died when he was just eight years old. I was blown away. It was a frozen moment for me. I had uncovered a family "curse," if you will. And this was a discovery that helped me to heal from the extremely negative perception that I had of my father. My father was not there for me. His father was not there for him. And his father's father had not been there for his father either. This knowledge helped me to stop blaming my father and *his* father too for that matter.

In that moment, I imparted the best words of wisdom I could come up with to get them to see the righteousness of each other's points of view but I didn't tell my father about the impact that conversation actually had on me until now, when I wrote this book.

The moral of the story here is- don't be afraid to ask your elders (especially your parents and grandparents) intimate details about your family tree. The answers could help you understand *your* life.

Self-Knowledge

I like to browse the book sections along sidewalk sales and was lucky to find inexpensive copies of: a book about astrology, a book about numerology and another book about the Myers-Briggs Type Indicator test. Each of these books contained all of the instructions to completing your own inventory assessments. The astrology book taught me how to identify my Sun, Moon and Rising signs as well as create my entire astrological chart, something that would have cost a minimum of $125 to have done by a professional astrologer. The numerology book was also a "do it yourself" guide to writing your own numerology profile. The Myers-Briggs Type Indicator test book is usually used in the workplace to assess a person's suitability to certain vocations. The book that I bought included the tests and results, which lead to a list of career paths that the user is suited for.

I found that the results of each of these self-inventories were consistent. Astrology, Numerology and the Myers-Briggs Indicator (which I have taken in a professional setting in addition to buying the book) all implied that I was a natural teacher, counselor and artist. To be more specific, my numerology report said that by this cycle of my life, I would learn the lesson of freedom, travel the world, change jobs, write and edit. Aside from writing this book, I have written business plans for start ups, proposals for non-profits and served as the Editor of what became a published book.

These inventories also detail the strengths and weaknesses that a person will have during his or her lifetime as well as the type of hobbies, causes and world views that they will be attracted to. I have found the results of these systems to be surprisingly accurate and even more surprisingly, consistent with each other.

Journaling

I used to keep a diary as a teenager but I didn't start again until I saw an episode of the Oprah Winfrey show where Oprah talked about the benefits of keeping a "Gratitude Journal." Easy enough. I got a small notebook and would write down what I was grateful for at the beginning of each day. Then I saw the same episode again a long time later and I noticed that Oprah said that she journals at the END of the day. And then it occurred to me that I could change up the way that I journal in order to make it more inspiring so that I would do it more often.

At first I would start off the top of the page with, "Today I Am Grateful For..." Then for a while I headed the page with, "Thank You Creator for..." After that I used, "I Have an Abundance Of..." "I Am Blessed With..." Every so often I come up with a new way to keep my journaling going. When I write in my journal, I feel uplifted.

90 Days of Forgiveness

A friend of mine, Dr. Anthony Smith, invited me to practice 90 Days of Forgiveness. I agreed to do it and marked the first day on my calendar so that I would know when it was over. My game plan was to be mindful about forgiving things and letting things go as I went about my daily life. He said it had 4 components:

1. Forgiveness starts in our own hearts. Only when we have forgiven ourselves can we give forgiveness to, or receive it from others.

2. Forgiveness is not conditional, even though our practice of it often is.

3. Forgiveness is an ongoing process. It continues in response to every judgment we make about ourselves and others.

4. Every gesture of forgiveness is sufficient. Whatever we are able to do now is enough. This understanding enables us to practice forgiveness with forgiveness.

This is one of those exercises where I went looking for one thing and found another thing. Spiritual work is often like that. You might work on one area of your life but get results in another area of your life that seems totally unrelated. As I started to practice the **90 Days of Forgiveness**, I found myself being more forgiving towards others and catching myself when I slipped into judgment. I experienced relief in the practice of forgiving myself along the way. I also found that I had a lot more forgiving to do than I had anticipated.

Practicing **90 Days of Forgiveness** showed me that I had been angry at "the system" in a certain kind of way. I was making it mean that the Foster Care system was the cause of all of the problems in my life. For many years, I felt that way. Through practicing **90 Days of Forgiveness** I came to an understanding that the truth of the matter was the system had taken care of me. I had been "a ward of the court" from the age of 4 on, until I was 21 years old, even though I had signed myself out of foster care at the age of 18. But that distinction enabled me to live a much better life than my parents could have provided, from my basic needs to my access to college. By the time that I would have naturally aged out of the foster care system, I was a college graduate.

It really helped for me to make a list of people that I needed to forgive. Seeing the list inspired me to take a moment and acknowledge each name, one by one to make sure that I had actually forgiven and not just swept their memory under the rug one more time. I also had a list equally as long of all the times that I needed to have some compassion for myself and forgive myself for acting out of character. I had practiced for a couple of extra weeks over the **90 Days of Forgiveness** by the time I checked my calendar. I realized that I could access this power of forgiveness anytime from then on and that it truly was a gift that I had given to myself.

Being of Service

I so loved having the weekend seminar experience that I have returned to their center on more than one occasion to volunteer as a coach for their new participants. One time I was asked to coach by the center staff and I agreed to do it although it had been about two or three years since I'd last visited the center. Once I got there, operations were not running smoothly and no one seemed to want to pull it together. The people that I came to help were upset about the overall disorganization and were gossiping about it on the sidelines instead of focusing on the participants. That negative energy started to get under my skin because I had to take directions from these disgruntled people. Let's just say that I "offered" to quit and go home early a few times but they wouldn't let me off the hook that easily.

It literally took eight people to coach me and to clear me so that I could coach four other participants. *What kind of math is that?* It felt like I was taking one step forward and two steps back. As each one of the "great eight" people generously took their time to work with me I realized that I was going to have to give some things up, or let some things go in order to connect with others.

What I was doing is called "being on it" and it seemed like so much more fun than "being off it" - while I was still "on it." But once I got "off it," I instantly felt lighter and more joyful. *Then* I was *eager* to be of assistance to others. When I was being "on it," I didn't want to be of assistance to others and my smile was upside down.

When I am being on it, I am being self-righteous at the expense of making someone else feel that they are just plain wrong. There is no way around it for the other party. My heart isn't flying or singing - it feels tense in those instances. When I am off it, the communication flows smoothly, more things get accomplished and the overall energy feels positive.

I ended up coaching the four participants on the very same issue that I needed to have a breakthrough in. It's called "getting off it." You have to actually "get off" the high horse that you rode in on before you can actually "be off" of it. I learned how to do that the hard way, the long way, the eight-coaches-in-a-row way. But hopefully, the participants that I coached will go on to touch other people's lives and in that way my four will multiply again and again like new life blossoming from scattered seeds.

The bliss of being of service is that it feels like you've stepped up, and made a difference in someone else's life, for a change. So much joy comes from helping others that it motivates me to do the next great thing that I can do to brighten someone else's day. That is the meaning of flying on the wings of love, that's how my heart feels when I am serving others.

Clearing Clutter as an Act of Generosity

Clearing clutter is a therapeutic activity on many levels. For one thing, you have to get physical. Even deeper, you get to clear your mind. I have noticed a symbiotic relationship between the organization of my home, including the closets, and my ability to focus on creative projects. I can't focus on sewing or painting if my house is not in order. One way to create space, physically and mentally, is to get rid of things that are not being used. Every so often, I donate my old books to the local library instead of throwing them in the trash.

I remember when a neighbor asked me to donate my used clothing to her church. She said that the donations would be shipped to Jamaica in a barrel. I vacationed in Jamaica a few years ago and had fond memories, so I agreed to help right away. It took me a few hours to go through all of my drawers and closets pulling out things that were too small for me, but were otherwise in good condition. I almost filled a black garbage bag with clothing. It was so heavy that I had to drag it across the floor all the way to her apartment.

I had to ring her bell a few times before she answered. She was an older woman in her forties or fifties and she had a traditional, thick, Jamaican accent. She was much shorter than me and very petite. Right away, I apologized for the heaviness of the bag. But she just slid the bag into her apartment and assured me that she was going to take a cab to her church the next morning with it. Well, we never discussed the donation again but sometimes when I would run into her on the elevator of our building she would be wearing articles of clothing from my legitimate "donation." Seriously, I would catch my neighbor all of the time wearing one of my old shirts here, a skirt there and occasionally even some of my old pocket books.

It's not my desire to embarrass anybody that is associated with the church. Yet I could not stop myself from looking her up and down whenever I did run into her. Although I never confronted her about the fact that she was wearing my donations to impoverished Jamaicans you wouldn't believe what she had the nerve to actually say to me! If logic had prevailed she would have *avoided* trying to make small talk with me but hey, I guess my neighbor is a bit of a firecracker.

We were in the elevator and she was shamelessly wearing one of the silk, black and white pin striped, button-up tops up that I had *donated*! She leaned towards me and said in her thick Jamaican accent "Yuh knowa, I wander when you were so skinny that yuh cuh fit into *these* clothes mon! *Wha happen to yuh*? Me feel so young whenna wear these clothes you gave me."

I was shocked and embarrassed that she said all of that to my face, especially when she knew damn well that I did not give her those clothes for her personal use. In the moment, I was more concerned with saving face by not letting her see that I was upset. I casually mumbled a few things about the fact that I had been a vegetarian for several years... She quickly snapped " Why yuh not doin that no more, eh?" I tried to explain it away: "I feel better now with more weight on me; I used to be cold and hungry all the time as a vegetarian; Now I just eat what I like so I'm happier." Now she was looking me up and down suspiciously until we exited the elevator.

I decided to suck it up and walk away instead of turning towards her and biting her head clean off the shoulders. It wasn't just *her* lucky day that I chose to walk away from a situation in which I knew that I was right. It was really *my* lucky day too. I could have made that 30 second elevator ride the longest, most awkward and judgmental ride that my neighbor has ever experienced. But at this point in my life, the act of being rude to someone else as a vengeful reaction was not an automatic impulse.

It is ok for me to give up being right even when I am right. I had gotten the benefit of clearing out my clutter and being generous at the same time. My work was done there.

Writing a New Script

Life is dramatic because it is riddled with contradictions. I used to freak out at the onset of a problem or conflict and the reactions I had were not always effective in bringing about resolutions. But I've learned that all contradictions can be resolved through communication. Change is normal. Growth is gained through challenge and adversity. In order to do this exercise "**Writing a New Script**" I had to take myself out of the center of every contradiction that bothered me. In other words, I had to become objective. It started with accepting that it's not my fault that life isn't picture perfect. It's ok that I don't always know what to say or do on cue. Life is unpredictable.

I can choose to review my life as a series of unfortunate events, or a comedy of errors. I could also choose to recall my life as a series of past events, current choices and future possibilities. In the next chapter I will write a brand new script to practice *giving myself* a fresh start.

Chapter 10: Living A New Story

Dear God, Teach me how to receive the world as an amazing, wonderful exploration playground full of mysteries and beautiful creations.

Earth's beauty is infinite from its heavenly bodies above, to its creatures at the bottom of the ocean below. God has chosen us to be on this huge playground and we can choose what to do within it. We can choose to play together and share our gifts or we can acknowledge the dark side and choose instead to focus on our physical differences or our differences of opinion.

Imagine a world where everyone operates from spirit and bases their actions on the principle of "the greater good." There would be no hidden agendas behind our interactions with each other. People could be easily felt and understood. Imagine how this could benefit society, businesses, and relationships at work and in schools. How we interact with each other in every area of our lives would be positively impacted if we operated from spirit.

How do we operate as a collective from spirit? Allow each person to make it their own experience. Then they'll become comfortable with having spiritual experiences through internal reflection. When operating from spirit, who you really are is on display. There is a smoothness and comfort in operating from spirit. If someone is not operating from spirit, you can feel, sense and know that the difference whether that person chooses to discuss it with you, or not. They can feel your energy too. Each human has a force field that is partly composed of emotional radiations. When we bump up against each other's force fields, we experience either attraction or repulsion.

What makes each person unique, special and different is that each person is the living expression of their own life's purpose. Through the Heart Point Meditation technique, our intentions become increasingly positive and impossible to conceal. If I can occupy my own heart then I can connect with the hearts of others.

While in a state of meditation, I learned that my purpose is to heal. What that looks like for me on a day to day basis, would be sticking to paths that reflect my purpose. My new plan involves exercise, the re-addition of fresh foods and maintenance of a thorough spiritual practice. I've lost 20 pounds over the past three months by exercising for 30 minutes a couple of times per week and by eating until I am satisfied and not full.

Eating until I am full is really overeating because then I am not able to move about freely until I have digested for a considerable amount of time. Eating until I am satisfied is physically realized as fullness about 10-15 minutes after I stop eating. The food sets in and I feel full and happy that I stopped myself at the point that I did because I am able to keep on moving after a satisfying meal.

I respect the fact that I have a weakness for certain types of bread, especially Italian bread, French bread, Portuguese bread and American breakfast rolls. I found it easier to enjoy these treats in moderation by taking a piece from the loaf and freezing the rest. This way, I can eat a serving of my favorite thing once or twice per week without feeling compelled to eat the whole loaf over the course of a couple of days before it expires. Fresh bread, once frozen, defrosts to its normal, edible state.

Another trick I have applied to losing weight is to brush my teeth when I get cravings for junk food. By changing the flavor of my taste buds with toothpaste, I lose the desire to eat what I thought I wanted to taste just moments before. Whereas I may have been craving chocolate, I find myself way more willing to snack on apples, pears and green grapes after brushing my teeth. Chewing on fresh, raw fruits and vegetables also contributes to the strength and appearance of whiter, brighter teeth in my experience.

Imagine if someone asked me now what my life has been like and I responded to them: "I am grateful to have been born to doting parents who instilled a strong sense of self in me from a young age. It was a huge blessing to be born in this day and age, in a place and time where there are organizations of generous folks who would take me in during my adolescent years. I thank God for answering my prayers by enabling me to become self-sufficient from the age of 18. Through the grace of God, I've built an extraordinary life for myself doing all of the things that I love to do for myself and others."

When I run down my list of accomplishments to other people and tell them that I have a master's degree, travel a lot, paint, make clothes and jewelry it sounds really good. I can say that I initiated and led a project where I turned an empty lot across the street from my building into a community garden, with the assistance of residents from my block. All of these things have been done with my intention to be a stable force for positive developments and changes inside of my own self and my community. But it's like so what, what is next?

How can I generate that feeling for life that makes it easy to get out of bed in the morning? What is a goal that would be worth reaching, that would give me the great joy of accomplishment? Can I out do the goals that I've already accomplished? That's a huge challenge but is it worth getting into if it's all about me? Just putting myself first, I know, brings me enough happiness and joy in life. Self-love and self-preservation are my divine orders.

I choose to see that I am blessed every day in every way. Life is a gift that God gives to each one of us as an opportunity to live and learn. You can choose to live by the rules and parameters of life or you can break the rules and deal with the consequences. If you are *really* living the high life you can even make your own rules. In this world, it seems like the ability to make your own rules come with a price. You can have all the freedom that your money can buy. If you can't afford your freedom, then you'll just have to work for it.

Through my relationship with God I have found freedom in doing the things that matter to me the most such as being of service, coaching others and creating art collections. I choose to be creative as I take in all of life's opportunities to grow and to learn. Life is a gift that can keep on giving or it can stop with me. It is still a gift nonetheless. What are you going to do with *your* gift?

Life is what you make it. What you put in, you get out. It is a total investment. You reap what you've sown. You could go to college and pursue a career. Or be an entrepreneur whose ideas are sold on the market. You can learn how to drive, swim, sew, sing, etc. You can learn to do anything that you want to do especially now that we live in the age of information (aka The Age of Aquarius.) You can go online and find out anything you want to know, right now.

I now realize that in order for my life to be worth living it has to be on purpose. Realigning with my purpose required me to recreate who I am not just in theory, but also in my ways of being towards others. I have to recall which values matter to me the most so that I can live into them. What I got down to is that I *have to impress myself in order to make my life worth living.* I would have to take actions that enabled me look at myself and say "I am an impressive person because I've impressed myself."

I can impress myself every day by doing the things that I love to do. The things that I love to do now are the same things that I always have enjoyed doing because they come naturally: Counseling others, creating art, seeking adventure, and of course staying on the spiritual path in every way possible. I am now choosing to live from my purpose, which is to heal, through my natural gifts and talents.

After more than a decade of solid work experience in these areas I finally CHOOSE to be an Author, Life Coach and Artist. I now have a Life Coaching practice where I counsel, inspire, motivate and most importantly HEAL my clients. Many of my sessions are conducted over the internet or the telephone. The sessions are very focused and designed to last an hour, yet I find that many clients choose to go into a two hour session so I always make sure to schedule plenty of time around each session so that there is no pressure to stop, there is only more space for the healing to continue.

Some of the services that I offer include: Counseling, Goal Setting, Mentorship, Guided Meditation, Art as Therapy and further instructions on how to practice the 13 Keys to Spiritual Power.

Based on my conversations with clients and friends, there seems to be a deep societal void where loads of healthy adults feel unsatisfied in the realms of sexual expression and sexual intercourse. To sum it up, people don't feel free to explore their sexual fantasies. My next writing project will focus on how this feeling of repression can potentially manifest into deviance from socially acceptable relationships.

The more energy that people put into freaking out over expressions of human sexuality, the more energy goes into the emergence of taboo sub-cultures. I am documenting what I've learned about these sub-cultures in a purely fictitious novel so that you won't have to physically experience the taboos yourself in order to know what's really going on in the world today.

Sexual relationships are of utmost importance because they can lead to child birth and/or parenting. As a small child, my biological parents had bought me the kind of toys that reinforced home economics like cooking, cleaning and mothering. I practically learned the meaning of life from the "Care Bears," whereas my older brother had toys that inspired him to go outside, explore and play. I had baby dolls and he had super hero action figures. I got a baby doll stroller and a plastic vacuum cleaner, with the little colorful balls in it that would pop up when you pushed it around, but he got a bike and with it a came a free pass to go outside and ride it. I've come a long way from being a little kid, trying to keep up with my older brother.

But I can't help but notice that women usually end up as mothers and homemakers (in addition to all of their other roles) while men usually end up hanging out with their male friends or pursuing their long term goals. Since so many people are dissatisfied with the status quo, I am currently fascinated by the concept of alternative lifestyles however unpopular they may be.

My only challenge now is to impress myself by living a purpose based life. As long as my thoughts, speech and actions are consistent with and in alignment with my purpose, I can achieve results. I used to build my life as a bridge to escape from the past. Once I got to the edge of it, all I could do was look back. Looking forward to the future was a fearsome task because I had not created for myself yet the next step that I was going to take forward, with the grace of God.

I needed to build a bridge to my future as opposed to continuing to build my bridge as a survival mechanism for the purpose of escaping the past. Looking back on my past, I built an amazing bridge and left behind me a very lush, green palace. Looking forward is now about acting on my true heart's desire.

If someone asks me "What are you going to do?" I won't automatically fall back on and rely on old fashioned, external views and references to my past behavior. How I will answer that question is directly proportionate to my degree of spiritual attunement, awareness of and alignment with my purpose. Being aware of your nature is going to give you the answer to that question for yourself. Allow your passion to be your compass.

I happen to be action oriented. Taking action is about self-motivation. Before I can jump out of bed with a renewable zest for life, I've first got to have big dreams. And so my advice to you is the same as it is to my self – KEEP ON DREAMING of new ways to express yourself. Sometimes life is about surviving for the purpose of telling your story.

Made in the USA
Lexington, KY
28 June 2014